Too Strong for Too Long

A SELF-LEADERSHIP MAP TO GUIDE YOUR JOURNEY

Sue Carr

Ark House Press
arkhousepress.com

© 2025 Sue Carr

All rights reserved. Apart from any fair dealing for the purpose of study, research, criticism, or review, as permitted under the Copyright Act, no part may be reproduced by any process without written permission.

Cataloguing in Publication Data:
Title: Too Strong for Too Long
ISBN: 978-1-7640298-2-7 (pbk)
Subjects: SEL021000   SELF-HELP / Motivational & Inspirational; BIO022000 BIOGRAPHY & AUTOBIOGRAPHY / Women; REL012070   RELIGION / Christian Living / Personal Growth.

Design by initiateagency.com

Contents

Dedication v
A Little About Me vii
Foreword ix

Chapter 1:   Too Strong For Too Long 1
Chapter 2:   Know Your Values 13
Chapter 3:   The Wheel of Life 34
Chapter 4:   Treasure Hunt Your Strengths 52
Chapter 5:   Get Comfortable In Your Own Skin 73
Chapter 6:   Celebrate Imperfection 86
Chapter 7:   How Big Is Your Why? 97
Chapter 8:   Fear Or Love 115
Chapter 9:   Thank You! Thank You! Thank You! 131
Chapter 10: Eye on the Prize 149
Chapter 11: Celebrate You 158

A Final Word of Encouragement 165
About the Author 169

Dedication

This book is for Andy, the man who has stood beside me in all the phases of our lives together. This book is for my children and grandchildren, whom I love beyond measure. This book is for the many special people who have shared their knowledge, insights and wisdom with me over the course of my life. I believe you know who you are. This book is for people everywhere, young and old, who want to live their lives with purpose, passion, confidence and joy.

A Little About Me

Hello, my name is Sue. I live happily on the Mornington Peninsula in Victoria. I am a woman who is proud of her growth and achievements through the ups and downs of life. I am a partner to my husband of 45 years. He is my greatest encourager and supporter.

I am the mother of five wonderful adult children who teach me about life and love each and every day. I am a grandmother to nine beautiful kids who absolutely light up my life. I am a teacher, a principal, and a transformation coach.

I love to write. I love to speak. I love to support others through coaching and mentoring. For relaxation, I cook, I spend time at the beach and I absolutely love to make things and spaces beautiful.

I am proud of who I am, and I am proud of the woman I am still becoming. This, my first book, is very special to me. I have carried it in my heart for such a longtime before it ever became words on a page. In this book, I have taken some elements of my life to share with you as examples of how I have learned to grow, to challenge myself, and to change.

I will share with you some of my times of confusion, doubt, overwork, and struggle that led me to experience burnout eight years ago.

With this book, I hope to show you that change and transformation are always possible, particularly if you develop a personalised map to guide your journey. I will share with you some of the elements of Positive Psychology, which is the art and science of human flourishing.

I will share with you some great coaching questions you can ask yourself as you embark on your own journey of personal transformation. I will share with you the simple tools, questions and actions that have helped me on my journey towards greater progress, success, fulfilment and happiness.

These tools, questions and actions have lit my path and have become both the signposts and the guiding lights on my journey through life. They have become my self-leadership map.

Foreword

> *"Owning our story can be hard but not nearly as difficult as spending our lives running from it. Embracing vulnerabilities is risky but not nearly as dangerous as giving up on love and belonging and joy – the experiences that make us the most vulnerable. Only when we are brave enough to explore the darkness will we discover the infinite power of our light."*
>
> Dr Brene Brown

Do you ever think about the events, decisions, challenges and opportunities that have led you to where you are now? Think about the life you've lived so far. How does it measure up in your own estimation? Is it exactly as you'd imagined or do you sometimes hear a whisper or a roar that says to you, "There must be more"?

Let me tell you:

> There is more.
> You are more.
> You are not too young.
> You are not too old.
> It is not too early.
> It is not too late to start.

We all want to live full, beautiful and rewarding lives. This takes awareness and commitment. It takes self-leadership in the form of a very brave heart to step into your personal brilliance; the brilliance that is your birthright.

Obviously, you've had moments and challenges where you thought that your life must consist of more. Can I tell you that it absolutely does? Sometimes in the midst of chaos, boredom, deep sadness, or just the daily grind, it can be difficult to find the path to greater happiness, satisfaction and freedom. In these times, you may need a confidante, an adviser, a cheerleader, or a coach.

You may simply need to take the time to really define who you are, why you are here and just how to step into your own personal power.

You want to be able to take a step out of the confusion, breathe, look up and recognise your birthright. You are a living treasure. You are a work of art. Every experience, every joy, every challenge, every thought has led you right to where you are today – to the day where you start to take charge, where you take hold of the wheel and begin to chart your own course. The course of your life; the life you are meant to live.

You are worth the investment.
Only you can design a life that is different.
Why waste another moment living an inauthentic life?
It's time to step into the really exciting space of self-leadership.
It's time to step up, step out, and be you!
If you can dream it, you can do it.
It's time to crack your personal brilliance code.

With love and gratitude.
Sue

Chapter One
Too Strong For Too Long

The Back Story

"Your present circumstances don't determine where you can go; they merely determine where you can start."

Nido R Qubein

In November 2017, I visited my doctor and told her that I was experiencing an anxiety that was terrifying me. I told her I was exhausted and that I couldn't possibly face going back to finish the year at the school where I worked as principal. I was a mess. I was a walking emotional wreck.

I sat in my doctor's surgery in a panic that completely overwhelmed me. My doctor looked at me with sympathy, but also with surprise. She said that I didn't sound like the woman she had come to know over many years. I began to cry. I cried deep, sad, exhausted tears. I was terrified. I didn't understand exactly what was happening to me. I was experiencing blurred vision, and the disconcerting feeling that my face looked distorted and strange.

I found myself constantly locking the doors in my own house to ensure my safety. I dreaded the nightly panic after my husband fell asleep. Each night the deep fear that I couldn't move my legs in bed terrified me. I prayed desperate prayers as I lived through the dreadful panic that each breath would be my last. These thoughts, actions and behaviours were my constant companions in those terrifying late November and December days.

My doctor calmly explained to me that I didn't have to return to work that year if I didn't feel I could. She reassured me that I could, and probably should, stop work immediately. Instant relief swept over me. For a few brief moments, I felt safe. The feeling of safety was like a warm hug grounding me, and easing my overwhelming feelings of just wanting to run away. This feeling of safety was short-lived but, in that moment, I felt safe. I could breathe.

The year had been a particularly difficult one. My father was experiencing rapidly deteriorating health. Early investigations suggested Parkinson's disease. This idea was later dismissed by specialist doctors. Eventually, we came to learn that he was experiencing vascular dementia. That summer he had a massively unfortunate fall where he sustained a gash to his head, suffered immense shock, momentary loss of consciousness, disorientation and a subsequent period of delirium.

My mother was desperately trying to keep my dad from having to move into a nursing home. She was trying so hard to ease his fear around having to leave the life he was comfortable with, and that he knew so well. By trying to care for him at home, her stress levels were 'through the roof' and her moods were, understandably, unpredictable. Both the difficult situation she found herself in, and her fear, definitely impacted my brother, my sisters, and me.

As the oldest child, I had always felt an incredible responsibility to help wherever I could, and I had always tried to 'manage' everyone's emotions. In my rational mind, I knew that this was not possible but, in my heart, and through my fear, I hoped that I could.

At the same time, I was heavily invested in my work as a primary school principal. I was trying to manage several underperforming teachers, some particularly challenging students, and their unrealistic and often extremely difficult parents. My character traits generally make me a person of kindness, social intelligence and perspective. I was true to type. I thought I needed to keep everyone happy, and this was a huge part of my downfall.

As a perpetual people pleaser, I was caught in a trap where this desire was simply not sustainable. I couldn't see it. I couldn't see the wood for the trees. I thought if I just 'pushed through', worked extremely hard, and kept giving more and more, everything would eventually workout.

Physical and mental exhaustion were my constant companions. Weight gain, digestive issues, skin irritation, and insomnia, were some of the results of my burnout. I had hit rock bottom. If not absolute rock bottom, as close as I ever wanted to be. How did I get to this lonely place of anxiety, exhaustion and fear? The only answer I had was that I had been too strong for too long.

I had always been ambitious, a people pleaser, and someone who, upon reflection, was desperately trying to prove to herself, and to the world, that she was enough! The eldest of five siblings, I had predominantly been a sensible and responsible child. However, in 1975, my world spun in a frighteningly different direction. I found myself in my final year of school, 17 years old, alone and pregnant.

After spending three months in complete fear, and having told nobody about my situation, I came to the realisation that I had a massive decision to make. At the tender age of seventeen, after a very honest yet supportive conversation with my mother and father, I decided to leave school and to have my baby. Although I was brilliantly supported by my loving parents, I was making a decision that would completely change the course of the life I had planned. From that point onwards, my maturity and my pride drove me to consistently try to demonstrate to others that 'I was fine', that I could manage, and that I would cope.

In November 1975, I gave birth to the most beautiful baby boy. My love for him was instant. He became my 'everything'. That year, and that decision, led me into a time of great challenge and great change. On the day of the Year 12 English exam, when most 17-year-olds were worrying about doing well in their final assessments, I was in a local hospital giving birth to my first son. This beautiful little boy provided me with the impetus to begin to create a very strong and secure family environment, that was warm, loving and safe.

I knew I had the support of my family, but I also knew that I was creating a family of my own. With this idea strongly embedded in my mind, it is important to state that the difference between my friends and I became extremely pronounced. Before my pregnancy, I had planned to travel to Europe with two of my closest friends after we had completed our final year of schooling.

It became obvious to me that my decision to be a mother to my baby meant that many of my previous dreams and plans were no longer relevant, important, or possible. On the day my friends left on their exciting European adventure, I was truly happy for them, but I absolutely felt the sting of being different and of missing out on what, I believed, would be the trip of a lifetime.

Fast forward seven months and, at the age of eighteen, I began a relationship with the boy who would eventually become my husband. Our attraction was strong. We shared similar interests and, in the golden glow of young love, we believed that anything was possible. We were going to be together. We were going to be fine. In reality, we were so very young, financially unstable, and just doing our very best to make a family. He loved my baby as his own. He loved me beyond measure, and I loved him.

We have faced many challenges in our 49 years together. It was not always easy to be consistently mature, responsible parents, when everyone around us seemed to be living the carefree lives they expected and had planned. Some of the challenges we faced together have been quite significant in the scheme of what life can serve up. I must emphasise, though, that we have also experienced many delights and many joys in our lives together. We have learned how to make the most of moments and of small things. Our greatest collective achievement is definitely the beautiful family we have created together. Five beautiful children, and nine absolutely precious grandchildren to date.

During the very busy years that we were raising our children, I finally 'stepped into courage' and commenced tertiary study. This was an ambition that I had long entertained. Yet, since I became a mother, it seemed that there was always something that held me back. Sometimes, it was the busyness of raising our family, at other times I believe that it was fear of the unknown. It had always been my plan to gain a tertiary qualification and to become a teacher. As time went on, and I became more fully entrenched as a mother and a 'housewife', I began to wonder whether that day would ever actually eventuate. Then, at the age of 33, an opportunity that I never expected was placed in front of me. It was an opportunity that I knew I couldn't let pass me by, so I finally stepped up and began to study for the education degree I had waited so long for. It was such an exciting step for me into the world of university life, and back to the world of really stimulating and sometimes, very challenging formal learning.

At university, I very quickly realised that I was in a place where I belonged. Having enrolled in a smaller institution, namely Christ College, in Chadstone, Victoria, soon to become known as Australian Catholic University, I pretty quickly became aware that I was in a place where I knew I could do well. The smaller, more intimate feel of the institution gave me the opportunity to connect easily with lecturers and tutors. The laid back, friendly atmosphere, and the positive energy, made me feel confident and, even though I was a mature age student, I felt quite at home.

At the time I began my studies, we had five children; a 12-year-old, who was rapidly becoming a teenager, and four little ones aged six and under. Needless to say, these were very busy, sometimes challenging, yet extremely rewarding years. With the support of my amazing husband and family, it took me five and a half years to complete my degrees.

In 1997, I was extremely proud and excited to gain employment as a full-time teacher at a Catholic primary school located about thirty minutes' drive from my home in bayside Melbourne. I instantly loved the role of teacher. I loved my work, and used the knowledge and skills I had developed as both a student teacher and as a mother, to engage my students and to confidently build trust with their parents.

I grew in confidence with each passing year, and leapt at every opportunity offered to learn and grow. I am continually grateful for the wonderful mentor and principal who first employed me. She must have seen something in me that I had not been able to see in myself. I believe she saw my enthusiasm, and my willingness to be involved and to learn new things. I tried to demonstrate from the outset that this was my long-awaited dream, my opportunity and my chance to make something of the late start to my career.

Each and every day I tried to show that I planned to progress quickly, to work very hard, and to do well. This was exactly what I did. I applied for middle leadership roles in my first school and then, after my huge disappointment at not being appointed Deputy Principal of the school that I loved so much, I accepted the outcome and continued to work hard until the next opportunity presented itself.

With courage, determination and a strong growth mindset, I continued to make my mark as a teacher and as a middle leader. In 2007, a new principal had arrived to lead the school and, as a new school year rolled around, I was faced with the prospect of doing exactly the same job for the next twelve months. I decided it was time for me to take things into my own hands and make the next move. Deep inside me I knew that if I wanted things to change, the next move had to be made by me. It was abundantly clear that things weren't going to change in my current workplace and so, once again, I stepped out of my comfort zone and applied for a new role in another school.

Before long, I was appointed as Deputy Principal at a new school closer to Melbourne and I embraced change with some trepidation, but eventually with courage and with joy. After almost five years, honing my skills and learning and growing every day, I decided it was time to try to make my next career move.

It was in my nature to want the 'top job'. I wanted to be a principal. I wanted to lead others and I knew, deep in my heart, that I wanted to demonstrate that I had climbed the mountain. I wanted to demonstrate to myself, and to the world, that the frightened, pregnant 17-year-old of 1975 had arrived! I wanted to show everyone, but especially myself, that I was not stupid or thoughtless or careless.

I had worked very hard and I had achieved a long-held dream. After two unsuccessful attempts, I was appointed to a small school on the Mornington Peninsula. I was delighted. I was over the moon. I had done it! I had reached a highpoint in my career. I was about to lead my very first school.

Life moved on, and so did I, after those dark days of burnout that brought me to my knees in late 2017. I returned to my work in the new school year, stronger, more able, and more determined than ever to find a healthy balance between my work and the rest of my life. My recent experiences taught me about the absolute importance of self-care, and of setting appropriate boundaries so that I could maintain a more manageable work/life balance. I realised that I needed to create more space for myself. I needed to strongly differentiate between 'my life' and 'school life'. I needed to establish some important personal boundaries. I had to learn that I could no longer 'spread myself too thin' and just assume that I would stay buoyant, high functioning and healthy.

During that time, I worked hard to learn to create more time and space for the things that were important to me outside of my professional life. I realised and accepted that the work I do as a school principal can affect me deeply. I realised that I needed to always have my wellbeing at the forefront of my mind. I also knew that, as a loving and caring partner, mother, grandmother, daughter, sister, and friend, that there would always be situations that would arise from time to time that cause me to worry.

Through lived experience, I also knew that the challenging times often require me to give a great deal of encouragement, love, support, and advice to others. I realised more profoundly than ever that, before I was able to help, support or comfort anyone else, I needed to take extra care of myself. I realised that in order to help others, I needed to 'fit my own oxygen mask first!' I realised that I was responsible for the personal boundaries I set, and for how I managed my own life.

After several visits with my doctor and a psychologist, and with the assistance of a short course of medication, I gradually felt my anxiety begin to ease. My physical exhaustion was still present, but the time I spent away from my work gave me the much-needed space and perspective to begin to look at my life anew. I began to gently apply, in a consistent and methodical way, some of the self-care strategies I had learned throughout my studies into human functioning.

Not all of the approaches that I used in my recovery were my own, they were simply tried and true ways of thinking and being that promote clarity, resilience and wellbeing. I have simply written about them in my own words in the sincere hope that other people may relate, find them useful and, perhaps, even use the journal pages I have designed as part of this, my first book.

With this new learning and way of being in mind, I began the 2018 school year full of optimism and readiness to begin. I was certain that I was going to lead myself and others in a positive and life-giving direction. It was to be an exciting new year. Our only daughter, and the baby of our family, was to marry the man of her dreams in early March.

Four days out from the wedding, I was leaving a meeting at a local school. I walked down the path basking in the glorious afternoon sunshine when, out of nowhere, my life was disrupted. I tripped, hitting my face hard on the pavement and putting my arms out to break my fall. I lay on the path in immense pain and shock. I felt tears rolling down my face. I touched it and saw on my fingers the blood from the grazes. All I could think of was how badly hurt I was, and about the wedding!

As I gingerly got myself off the footpath, I tried to decide whether to walk back to the school office to ask for help, or to drive myself back to the school where I worked, which was just eight hundred metres away. Not wanting to 'make a scene', and not wanting to ask for help, I decided to try to drive back to school. I got into my car, started it and attempted to turn the steering wheel. This is when I knew that at least one wrist was broken. I steered my car back to school with my left hand.

As I drove into the school car park, waves of nausea hit me along with waves of relief that I had actually made it back. I was attended to by caring colleagues, and taken to hospital. It soon became clear that I had broken two bones in my wrist, and shattered the joint. I had severely bruised my other hand, grazed my face, and buckled the cartilage in my nose. The thing that shocked me most was the shock itself. How is it that life can creep up on us, and blindside us in ways and at times we least expect?

For many weeks after the wedding, as I healed from the physical injuries and basked in the afterglow of the beautiful family celebration that I had been privileged to be part of, I reflected on how quickly and surprisingly life can pull us up short, make us stop and realise that things so often don't go according to plan. We never really know what's just around the corner, so we need to work always to develop ourselves as strong, resilient people who live with a growth mindset, especially when faced with the inevitable challenges that life will present us.

My strong realisation post-accident was that I was still far more fragile from my burnout than I had initially realised. I was fragile, sensitive, and so willing to lap up any small act of kindness or care that was offered to me. What was it in me that made me think that I had to present myself to the world as 'bullet proof'? Why did I find it such a challenge to give myself the 'permission to be human'?

Throughout 2018, I watched as my father's health further declined. To his fear and disgust, he became a resident in a local nursing home. This change brought some relief and respite for my mother who had fought so valiantly to keep him at home. She had been so doggedly determined to keep him with her where he wanted so desperately to remain. My brother, sisters and I had worked hard to support our parents' wishes but, in the end, it became obvious that this was beyond our collective abilities. Once again, I realised that it was time to give myself the permission to be human. I needed to care for, and create space for, myself as I watched my father's quality of life slip further and further away.

On January 14, 2019, while I was attending a leadership meeting at school, my beautiful dad died after his long and difficult battle with vascular dementia. This was another life changing moment when I realised that self-care was of the utmost importance. I needed to look after myself, and to find the time and the appropriate ways to remember my father and to grieve his loss. It was also a timely reminder to cherish and nurture the people and the things I love most. It was time to wrap my arms around my family, and to allow them to embrace and support me as we moved forward, forever changed by our experiences and by our loss.

Later that year, I was extremely proud to gain a formal qualification as a growth coach. I adore this work and I truly appreciate and recognise its immense value and the impact it can have on the lives of those who choose to embrace it. I was able to employ many of the skills I had learned to support myself and others in my family during this very sad time.

My confidence with people has always been my strong suit. I love meeting people. I love teaching, speaking, writing, presenting, and coaching. Over the course of my career, and my life in general, I have possessed an inner knowing that my profound interest in people is what drives me to connect with them, and to know what moves and motivates them. Personal development and 'inner work' intrigue me. I have always craved it for myself, and I have found that I can use the skills I have developed through my studies in Positive Psychology, Leadership, Wellbeing, and Growth Coach training, to connect and deeply engage with others.

I have chosen to share some of the personal elements and anecdotes from my life as an introduction to this book, simply to illustrate that anyone can reach a point in their life when they begin to question their choices, decisions and, sometimes, even their sanity. There are many people with all sorts of challenges, often far greater than mine, who pick themselves up and dust themselves off and start over time and time again. I have deliberately not shared some of the most intimate and challenging parts of my life because they are other people's personal stories, as well as my own. In my efforts to be strong, I have learned that we are all works-in-progress. I strongly believe that we must nurture ourselves so that we can nurture others. And, above all, I know that ultimately life is good when we take responsibility for our own growth, wellbeing, and happiness. It is my heartfelt hope that I can convey to others just how beautiful life can be amid the challenges it inevitably throws at us.

Chapter Two
Know Your Values

Your Internal Compass

"Your core values are the deeply held beliefs that authentically describe your soul."

John C. Maxwell

The longer I live, the more I believe that living a life that is guided, directed and bound by a personal set of values, is a truly rewarding one. Values have provided me with the direction, and the boundaries, from which I live an authentic and purpose-driven life.

I realise that when my values are formed through the alignment of the head (my intellect), the heart (my emotions) and the gut (my instincts), they help to shape my personal map for living. The feelings, reactions and responses we experience in our heads, hearts, and guts, help to keep us on our personal pathway towards our desired outcome, destination or goal.

As we journey through life on this planet, whether we recognise it or not, we are searching for our 'true north', our purpose, our reason for being. We want to know why we are here. Values form the foundational structure that help to keep us grounded and 'on course' throughout our lives. Values serve every person who strives for a greater, more effective, and more fulfilling style of self-leadership.

Many years ago, I attended a seminar led by Craig Harper, a well-known and highly respected Melbourne-based speaker, trainer, researcher and coach. Craig asked a brilliant question of his audience. He asked: "Who was flying our plane?" The question has stuck with me over many years and, since then, I have asked myself that very question on more than one occasion. I have come to realise, through sometimes bitter experience, that a values-driven life best serves those who want to 'drive their own bus' or 'fly their own plane'. A values-driven life puts you in the driver's seat. It puts you in control.

Values are like the guard rails on a freeway or the points on a compass. They lead, direct, and guide us, to where we innately know we need to go. They keep us moving in the direction of our true purpose. When we live in alignment with our values, we are moving in a direction that serves our personal growth and development. When we take care of, and responsibility for, our own growth and development in a manner that is in alignment with our values, not only do we benefit, but often we also contribute to the common good of our families and our communities.

My values have served me many times, especially in some of the highly challenging moments of my life. Even when my days are less remarkable, my values serve me so that I can show up each day as the best version of myself.

Every important decision that I have made in my life has ultimately been sifted through the framework of my values. Even before I had thought about and named my values, and before I had developed a clearly articulated list, I still somehow innately knew whether my choices and decisions sat well with me, or whether they made me feel uneasy, restless and unconvinced. I now know that this uneasy feeling was my inner voice tapping, nudging or sometimes screaming at me that my choices were not reflecting the true me.

I encourage you to ask yourself the following questions:

- **Am I a person who is searching for greater meaning, fulfilment, and joy in my life?**
- **Am I trying to build alignment between my head, heart and gut?**
- **Do I have a values list that I can clearly name, and that I can speak about with confidence?**
- **Do I own my values and live them each and every day?**

If not, in your quest for stronger self-leadership, I suggest that the development of a personal values list is a wonderfully intelligent and highly effective place to start.

I want this book to be authentic. I want it to be real. I want you to sense me in every part of it. So I ask myself: what are some examples from my life where I allowed my values to lead me?

Here is an example of how my values guided me when I was much younger. It occurred many years ago when I was studying to become a teacher. One night, while at a party, I met a man who spent a long time talking to me. He told me he was the creative director of a large advertising agency in Melbourne. He told me that my warmth, naturalness, self-confidence and ease with people, would make me an 'absolute natural' to work in the field of advertising sales.

He phoned me the following Monday morning and offered me an interview at a popular Melbourne radio station. I was, at that stage, extremely flattered and, I must admit, somewhat seduced by the offer. The prestige, the money, and the possibility of walking away from the daily grind of tertiary study were immensely appealing. Perhaps I would be able to earn a salary that would contribute to my family's financial wellbeing and ease the burden on my husband who worked six days per week. I thought that, perhaps, I would find myself a foothold in the glamorous world of advertising.

As I prepared for the interview, tried to decide what to wear, and drove to the radio station, my emotions swung wildly between excitement, nervousness, and a nagging doubt that something was not sitting quite right with me. I later realised that the doubt came from my inner voice. It was reminding me of my values. This job would certainly involve late nights, openings, product launches, and events, and work shifts that would possibly mean not being available to spend quality time with my family. After being offered the position and listening to the attractive starting offer, I felt more uncertain than ever.

Did I take the position? No. Did I understand why? Possibly. I just knew that something did not sit quite right with me. Many years later, when I learned about values and how powerful they can be in decision making, I realised that my values of family, love, and integrity, were guiding me on a different path. I listened to that voice, and I chose to continue with my studies and, eventually, become a teacher. The idea of the late nights and the many networking events I would need to attend, did not sit well with me while we were trying to raise our young family.

This is just one example of where my values spoke to me in an indirect way. They were alerting me to the fact that I was steering off course, away from my family and away from the value of love. This caused my integrity to alert me to the fact that I was possibly making the wrong decision.

> *"Values guide your behaviours, decisions and actions."*
> Shalom H. Schwartz

Now let me take you to one of the lowest points of my life. For many reasons, we found ourselves in the frightening situation when my husband's business was in real financial trouble. We were faced with the devastating news that we were going to lose our home. I was terrified of what lay ahead. There were many times I lay awake at night and wondered how I would possibly endure it. I absolutely despised watching my hard working, highly skilled, and honest husband suffer this major setback where his very identity, and our relationship, were called into question. I didn't want to worry our children, and have them watch us leave the home we had built together and where they had grown up. I was tired of the gossip mongers who took delight in saying they were, "Sure that she will leave him".

For myself, my ego and my pride were hurting. I crave security. I have always been strongly driven by the need to prove that I'm 'okay'. I know that material possessions are not everything but, when faced with losing something as important as our home, for me it was an absolutely terrifying experience. Everything that made me feel secure and confident was under threat. It felt as though the ground was falling away beneath my feet. My emotions swung wildly between fear, sadness, anger, resentment, and embarrassment. I did not enjoy the fact that my life felt out of control. Even more than this, I absolutely hated the fact that other people knew about it.

Whenever I could, I spent time alone, walking, thinking, crying, and praying. Amidst the pain and fear, I innately knew that I had to be strong. My inner voice kept nudging me, prompting me, and telling me that I had to try my hardest to be the glue that held it all together. I had to hold my family together. My values gave me the clue. They provided the guardrails that helped me to navigate my way through this truly difficult time.

Some of my values include:

- health and wellbeing
- family
- love
- optimism
- gratitude

I innately knew I had to take charge of whatever I could. So, with these values being both the guardrails and the guiding lights of my life, I set about consistently doing the following things:

- I took extra care of my health and wellbeing so that I had the energy to support my husband, and give love, quality time, and care to my family – I tried to eat well and not drink too much alcohol. I walked every day.
- I spent time making our home feel safe and welcoming for all the members of my family – I cooked healthy, delicious dinners. I ensured our home was clean and comfortable.

- I made sure that love was at the forefront of my words and actions. (I must admit, though, that sometimes I failed miserably!)
- I tried to take an optimistic view of my life beyond the dark place I currently found myself in – I visualised, and wrote a description of, the home we would one day own. I visualised our family and friends enjoying happy times together with us in that home.
- I made sure to say thank you often, and to appreciate the beauty that was still all around me. I made sure that I searched hard and looked deeply, to find things to be grateful for. As I went on my morning walks, I took stock of all that was still beautiful in my world – the beach, trees, flowers, birds, animals, clouds, and people. Taking time to notice all that was beautiful and still available to me helped create a softness in my heart. It helped me to experience moments of joy amongst the very many moments of sadness.

As I navigated my way through both of these very different situations, I didn't ever use the term self-leadership. I didn't know it yet. It was not in my vocabulary. What I do know is that my values called me to live and act in ways that helped me cope with very challenging situations, make difficult decisions and they also helped me to live through them.

Through my coach training, and my studies in both Positive Psychology and Wellbeing, I learned that values form the bedrock from which people live positive and meaningful lives.

> *"Values can't just be words on a page.
> To be effective, they must shape action."*
>
> *Jeffrey R. Immelt*

Now, I want to share with you the process I used to define my own personal set of values.

My Process – How did I create my personal values list?

This is my process for creating a meaningful list of values. I believe it is an effective approach. Please be aware, though, that it may take anywhere between a few hours, and a few days or weeks, before your list feels authentic, comfortable, and a good fit for you. If you would like to develop a list of your own personal values, I suggest you follow these action steps.

Your first self-leadership mapping task:

- First, write down any values that you already know that you'd like to include in your list.
- Next, find a list of values from which you can select other words that resonate with you – a simple 'Google search' will give you a multitude of lists from which to choose.
- You may like to use the list of values that I have included below.
- Read each of the values on whichever list you select.
- As you read each word, take a breath, and let the word sit with you for a while.

KNOW YOUR VALUES

- Take the time to see whether it resonates with you. See whether it feels authentic, and whether you could live that value every day.
- If a word resonates with you, write it down on a sheet of paper.
- Move through the list recording the values that resonate with you until you can list between 8 and 10 values that feel credible and authentic. They need to sit comfortably with you.
- Leave your list in a place where you can see it often throughout your day.
- Go back to your list from time to time – *you will find yourself thinking about the list while you are doing other things.*
- Add to, or delete from, the words you have recorded until the list feels authentic. It should feel like a comfortable pair of shoes.
- When you think you are satisfied, print the list or write it again, showing only the words that you want to include, then put it in a place or several places where you will see it often. *I suggest the bathroom mirror, the screensaver on your computer, the fridge door – wherever you feel comfortable to have your list displayed.*
- Read the list often. Try to commit it to memory so that you can name your values easily, wherever you are, whenever you like.
- Once you believe your list is a perfect fit for you, take some time to record why each value is so important. Think about each value, and write down your reason/s for making it part of your list.
- Finally, record real life examples of how you expect this value to show up in your life, and how it will be enacted by you in the big and small moments you experience.

My Values Chart

Love	Gratitude	Integrity	Wellbeing	Security	Optimism
Kindness	Creativity	Health	Freedom	Hope	Vitality
Courage	Connection	Self-Reliance	Diligence	Curiosity	Respect
Humour	Resilience	Faith	Compassion	Empathy	Solidarity
Teamwork	Growth	Learning	Reliability	Peace	Vulnerability
Leadership	Contribution	Confidence	Variety	Family	Friendship
Persistence	Professionalism	Service	Trust	Intelligence	Humanity
Passion	Purpose	Meaning	Accomplishment	Generosity	Joy

My Personal Values List:

Health and Wellbeing

Family

Love

Kindness

Integrity

Optimism

Gratitude

Creativity

Connection

Appreciation of Beauty and Excellence

KNOW YOUR VALUES

Here are three examples of how I wrote about the words in my values list:

> **Kindness** is the value that drives me as I live my life. It is the fuel that allows me to move forward in a way that makes me feel proud of who I am, and of how I show up in the world.
>
> I ask myself each day, *"How will I, as a person who has kindness as a central value, respond to the people I meet today?"*
>
> My answer is that I will respond to each person I meet with interest, warmth, and a ready, willing and open smile. I will choose my actions and responses with a kind heart. I know that kindness makes others feel seen and valued. I know that kindness makes me who I am. It lights me up from the inside.
>
> **Gratitude** is the lens through which I see the world. It keeps me grounded and real. I believe that living with an attitude of gratitude makes me a happier, more aware human being, who can find beauty and joy in even the smallest things. It even helps me in the times that are sad, lonely or challenging.
>
> I ask myself each day, *"How will I, as a person who has gratitude as a central value, show appreciation for the people I connect with, and the things that I experience?"*
>
> My answer is that I will take time to notice and celebrate nature, food, possessions, situations, and the people who show up in my life each day. I will express wonder, joy, and thanks for the things I have. I will be grateful for the things I notice, and the situations

I experience because, even though sometimes these things may be challenging or unpleasant, they all have something significant to teach me. They offer me things from which I can learn and grow.

Health and Wellbeing are central to being able to fully experience life. My body and mind combine to create the vehicle from which I navigate my life. It has taken time for me to fully appreciate just how central health and wellbeing are to every facet of the life I plan, the life I live, and to the life I want to enjoy. Vibrance, energy and ease, are elements of a healthy life. They are feelings I want to experience each and every day that I am alive.

I ask myself each day, *"How will I, as a person who has health and wellbeing as a central value, nurture my body, mind and spirit today?"*

My answer is that I do this by eating healthy, nutritious food, keeping my body well hydrated, exercising for strength, stamina, and general fitness. I take care of my mind, body and spirit by ensuring I relax and breathe deeply each day.

Self-Belief Statements

Once I had spent some time developing a list of values that spoke directly to my heart, I realised that I needed to create a set of personal belief statements that would make my values come alive.

A belief statement, that is written from your heart, allows you to adhere to and align with your journey towards becoming the best version of yourself. A personal belief system and set of beliefs statements are fundamental to the development and growth of your vision, values and mission. I like to call these 'self-belief statements' because, quite simply, they are statements you make about yourself.

My dive into the world of leadership, personal development, wellbeing, and coach training, has been both deep and profound. Therefore, developing a set of belief statements became my next important priority, and so I set to work writing a set of self- belief statements where each began with the words, 'I am'.

> *"Your beliefs become your thoughts, your thoughts become your words, your words become your actions, your actions become your habits, your habits become your values and your values become your destiny."*
>
> Mahatma Gandhi

My list of statements has changed over time. I think these changes reflect part of a natural progression. They are part of my growing up, and of becoming more mature. They reflect both my experience and my growth. They are aspirational statements. Each reflects who I am, or who I want to be, when I am at my best. My first list of self-belief statements was perhaps immature, and something of an overreach. I thought that they had to sound as though I could save the world, and sacrifice myself in the process!

After the dark days at the end of 2017 and early 2018, I came to realise that I needed self-belief statements that, first and foremost, served me and reflected my values. My self-belief statements form my mantra, my map, and my guide for living a life that reflects real self-leadership. My beliefs have my personal values for living deeply embedded within them.

I use these key statements every day to make choices and decisions. I also use them to help me set firm personal boundaries, and to prioritise myself. I do this so that I can show up every day as the very best, healthiest, most positive version of me. My beliefs support me to live a life of joy and fulfilment. They also help me connect with, and take care of, the people and things I love and value the most.

Beliefs are ideas or concepts that we hold as truths in our hearts and minds. Beliefs are a subset of values. It is important that I speak about them here, at the beginning of my book, because I know that when our beliefs are aligned with our values, our roadmap for navigating the world becomes clearer, and more illuminated. Values and beliefs provide us with a most compelling map to follow. I call this map the **self-leadership map**.

I have found it extremely helpful to develop a list of personal beliefs that I can recite as a mantra. Each morning, as I conduct the ritual of brushing my teeth, and cleansing and moisturising my face, I stand in front of my bathroom mirror with my feet placed firmly on the floor, my shoulders squared, and my body facing front onto the mirror. I make sure that I look deep into my eyes as I recite the statements. I take a deep breath, smile at myself, and repeat my mantra clearly, quietly and with confidence.

Please note that looking into my eyes as I recited my statements did not come easily or naturally to me. In the beginning, I found myself looking down at the bathroom vanity, or looking away to the side. I felt like a fraud saying these things to myself. Over time, my confidence and self-belief grew, and I found I could say the words and take courage and confidence with me as I stepped out to live a new day.

How did I develop my list?

I looked with positivity at myself, and at whom I knew I wanted to be in the world. In some moments of deep reflection, I cast off my doubts about myself. I let go of my inner critic who, from time to time, I have allowed to hold me back. I sat quietly and breathed deeply. I listened to my inner voice. I knew that my inner voice came from my heart.

My inner voice tells me that I am gifted, resilient, and capable. From this belief, I formed these statements:

- I am strong
- I am beautiful
- I am confident
- I am capable
- I am resilient
- I adapt to change and learn new things
- I treat myself with respect, care and kindness
- I treat others with kindness and respect
- I am a communicator
- I am a connector
- I am a writer
- I am a coach
- I learn and grow every day
- I am ENOUGH

How To Develop Your Own List.

I suggest you follow my process:

- Take time out just for you.
- Start to 'try on' different statements that you'd like to make about yourself.
- Link your self-belief statements to your values.
- Write each statement beginning with the words, 'I AM'.
- Write your statements onto a clean sheet of paper.
- Say them out loud.
- See how they resonate with you.
- Do they sound believable to you?
- Do your statements inspire you?
- See whether they are statements you can work with, practise and try on, just as you would a new pair of shoes.
- Ask yourself, "Do these statements excite me?"
- Do these statements ground you in the same way an anchor keeps a boat from coming adrift?
- Tweak and revisit your statements until they feel just right for you.
- You will notice that not all of my statements begin with 'I AM'. If you want to add any other statements, include them in your list.
- Your list does not need to be as long as mine. You may choose to have three or four statements. Your head, heart and gut will guide you.
- Set them as a wallpaper or screensaver on your phone, computer, or vision board.
- Use them as a tool, or a fuel, to propel you on your daily journey through life.

Once my statements became a mantra and a daily message to myself, I found that my practice evolved from simply standing in front of the bathroom mirror and repeating my beliefs, to something even more worthwhile. I had the opportunity to work with Shannah Kennedy, the wonderful Melbourne-based coach whose work I had admired and followed for a long time.

Shannah shared with me the idea of using 'mirror breaths'. As we know, the simple act of breathing deeply and slowly, allows us to become calm. When we engage in this type of breathing, we gain access to clearer thinking, and to our highest selves. In this space, we find courage, clarity and confidence. Research tells us that *"Breathing deeply activates the hypothalamus, which connects the nervous system to the endocrine system – the system that controls and regulates hormonal activity. The simple act of inhaling and exhaling slowly blocks stress hormones and produces a calming physiological effect."*

Shannah Kennedy also shared with me the interesting idea that each time we use the bathroom, we can take a private moment to oxygenate our body, and to calm and centre our mind and spirit. She suggested that a person may use the bathroom around six to eight times per day. She explained the simple and wonderful opportunity we have, for a moment in that private space, to take some deep, cleansing breaths to calm, centre and renew ourselves.

I liked the sound of this idea, and I found myself playing around with taking three deep, cleansing breaths each time I was in the bathroom. As with anything we become conscious of and begin to practise, this action soon became second nature. I found that within a few weeks, I had become a regular 'bathroom breather'! Soon after, I expanded my practice to include quietly reciting my self-belief mantra just after I had taken three deep breaths.

This practice has now become automatic. I find that it helps me to feel more balanced, in control, and to live well. It helps me to live with courage, strength and conviction. It reminds me daily of just who I am, and it helps to reinforce in my mind and heart just how I want to show up in the world. The combination of slow, deliberate breathing, and the recitation of my belief statements, helps me face the world with courage, confidence and authenticity.

I don't enjoy conflict or drama. I find myself avoiding it at all costs. When I know that I am going to be in a potentially challenging situation, particularly in my work as a primary school principal, I have found that my self-beliefs' practice helps me to manage conflict, and be prepared for the occasional challenging conversation or outpouring of emotions (sometimes angry or frustrated ones) that may come my way. I'd like to mention that occasions, such as these, do not occur too frequently but, when they do, they can leave me surprised and shaken at how some people express discomfort, displeasure or concern.

An example of this type of unpleasant encounter occurred in the early days of my principalship. I was dealing with a situation where two boys had been involved in a playground fight that, as far as primary school students are concerned, was actually quite serious. Naturally, both parents were keen to defend their children. I had held several meetings where I'd spoken with each parent separately. What I didn't realise at the time was that the two parties had a recent disagreement of their own. Of course, the lingering bad feelings between them had caused their actions and reactions, in response to the fight between their sons, to become, at times, rude, aggressive and highly inappropriate.

One afternoon, I was meeting with one of the parents when my office manager came to inform me that the other parent was waiting at the reception area to see me. I concluded the meeting with the first parent, and advised them to leave by another door to avoid a likely scene. When I opened my door to invite the other parent into my office, I was met with a torrent of abuse. This particular parent abused me using some very colourful language. Let's just say that their language was totally inappropriate. I was shocked, not because I'd never heard such language before, but because I was unaccustomed to being spoken to in such an aggressive manner. From somewhere deep within me, I responded by firmly saying, "If you want to speak with me, I will be in my office when you feel ready to have a respectful conversation". With that statement, I turned, walked back into my office and closed my door.

With everything in me, I wanted to avoid the interaction that was about to occur. However, I also knew that this was an impossible outcome, so I took three of the deepest, most centring breaths that I could manage. I sat down at my desk, composed myself further, and waited for a short time. After a couple of minutes, there was a quiet knock on my door. I chose not to stand to open it. I simply said in a calm yet firm voice, "Come in". I remained behind my desk to create a visual and physical barrier between us. I wanted to send a clear message that I was in control of the meeting. I wanted to send a message, to myself, that I was in control of my reactions and responses.

At that stage of my life, I didn't have a series of belief statements to support me yet, somehow, I knew that slowing my breathing and becoming fully present was the most positive way to manage myself in this challenging situation. After this awkward meeting concluded, I was left somewhat shaken. I felt attacked for carrying out my role in the very best way I knew. My human nature, and my need to protect myself, made me think of how I might avoid being in such a situation again. It made me think about what I would do differently if ever such a situation arose.

In the days after this angry outburst, I realised that I should take proactive steps to protect myself against the poorly managed emotions of others. I realised that, if possible, I should have a colleague close by when conducting such a meeting. I realised that I could always conclude a meeting at any moment. I also realised I could use my voice to clearly state my case.

More recently, as my belief statements ritual evolved, I can honestly state that this practice helps me believe in myself, and in who I tell and show the world that I am, each and every day. The work I have done to define, practise and live by my values and my belief statements has helped me immeasurably over the past decade. I believe that the following formula provided me with a perfect tool to add to my self-leadership map:

KNOW YOUR VALUES

Self-Leadership Map Signpost No:1
Values + beliefs + breath = a stronger, more confident, more resilient you.

Great Coaching Questions About Beliefs and Values
Can you name your values and self-belief statements?
What action are you taking every day to live your values, and to enact your self-belief statements?

A Piece of Wisdom from Positive Psychology
Understanding our values can help us live a life that is more meaningful and in alignment with what we desire and believe is right. According to psychologist Russ Harris, it is important to understand that values are not the same as goals. A value is not something that you can just cross off or achieve. Instead, it is something that you continuously aim to live and move towards.

Chapter Three
The Wheel of Life

How Balanced Are You?

"When you have balance in your life, your work becomes an entirely different experience. There is a passion that moves you to a whole new level of fulfilment and gratitude, and that's when you can do your best ... for yourself and for others."

Cara Delevigne

Balance, structure, rhythm and momentum all add a sense of security, meaning and purpose to our lives. These elements help to make us feel more surefooted and confident on our journey. They help to keep us on the road to progress, achievement, success, and fulfilment.

There are many facets to the lives we live. We all play a variety of roles – parent, child, partner, sibling, manager, employee, friend, coach, teacher, leader, etc. We all have needs. The need for:

- Security
- Significance
- Purpose
- Health
- Creativity
- Recognition

and the list goes on. The roles we play, and the many facets of our humanity, all contribute to making our lives satisfying and worthwhile. When our needs are met, they help to keep us nourished, stimulated, fulfilled and, ultimately, high in wellbeing. I believe that we all have needs in the following areas of our lives:

- Health
- Family
- Relationships
- Personal Growth
- Social Life
- Career
- Finance

When these needs are unmet, or out of balance, life navigation becomes really difficult. It is as though we are moving on auto-pilot, simply accepting the status quo as 'just our lot in life'. We may find ourselves trying to navigate the path of our lives on wheels that are out of alignment, or on tyres that are flat or set at different rates of pressure.

> *"How can we expect to experience a smooth ride when at least one of our tyres is flat?"*

This is an important self-leadership question. It was certainly one I had to ask myself when I became so unwell and was experiencing burnout just a few short years ago. In my people-pleasing, perfection-seeking style, I had absolutely neglected many elements of my physical and emotional health, and wellbeing. Looking back, it is so easy to see what I did, and didn't do well enough, to look after myself:

- I didn't always live up to my values in ways that supported me.
- I didn't have a set of belief statements that guided and served me.
- I didn't set clear boundaries that guided me in my relationships with others.
- I let my work, and some of the challenges within my family, dictate my life.
- I didn't say 'no' often enough.
- I let myself become empty, overwhelmed, and exhausted.

One of my favourite sayings in life is that 'You cannot draw from an empty well'. That is exactly what I had been trying to do for many years.

Finally, my well was almost dry. I didn't realise this, and my body was clever in its attempts to protect me. It sent me so many signals that I ignored. I stopped exercising. I gained weight. I didn't eat or drink as healthily as I knew I should. I didn't sleep well. I worked too hard and too long each day. I didn't set or respond to my 'off switch'! There was little protective and restorative 'down time'.

If any of these behaviours resonate with you, may I suggest that you try some self-care? Take the time to regularly check in on yourself. Take stock and conduct an audit on just how well you are looking after yourself.

First, check in on your values. See how much of your life is actually lived in alignment with them. For example, if one of your values is health and wellbeing, what are you doing on a daily basis to promote and live that value?

Next, look at your belief statements. Does the life you are currently living reflect these beliefs? If you haven't yet developed lists of values and beliefs, I believe that now is an excellent time to start. You can do this on your own using the steps outlined in this book, or with the help of a mentor or coach.

> *"Balance is not something you find;*
> *it is something you create."*
>
> Jana Kingsford

When reflecting on the progress and balance in my own life, I like to use a wonderful tool called the 'Wheel of Life'. I use this tool once each season, or quarter of the year, for my own self-reflection. I also use it with my coaching clients. This tool can be found by conducting a simple search on your computer. You may find that the headings for each segment of the wheel vary from one example to another. I have shown below the one I like to use.

The Wheel of Life

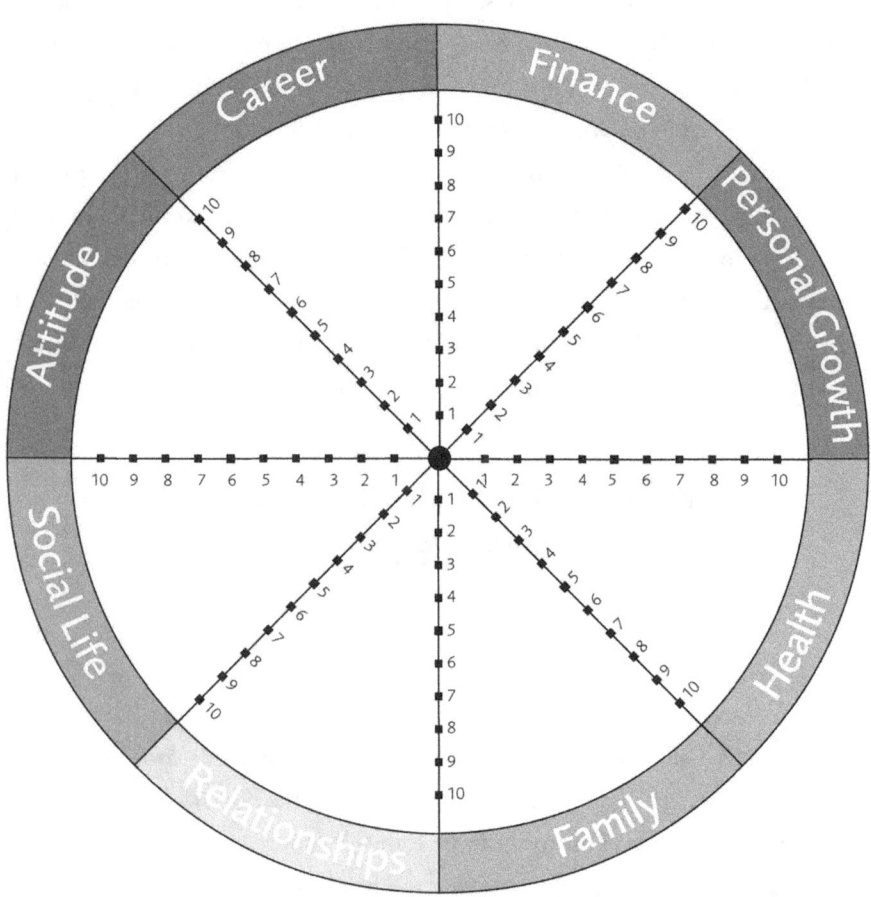

THE WHEEL OF LIFE

How to Use the Wheel of Life.

- Look at all the headings and decide which segment of the wheel you will reflect upon first.
- It may be the one where you feel you are experiencing the most success in your life.
- It may be the one where your heart instinctively knows you need to direct your attention.
- Sit quietly, breathe in and out, then ask yourself, how am I tracking in this important area of my life?
- Use the rating scale of between 1 and 10 to indicate where you feel you currently are in relation to that aspect of your life.
- Decide on a number and draw a line across from one side of the segment to the other.
- Once you have graphed each segment, and your wheel is complete, take a close look at it. What shape is it? Are you driving through life on a wonky, misshapen wheel? So many of us do and we wonder why we struggle to gain traction, build momentum, and move forward with a positive sense of ourselves.
- Look at your wheel again, see where you are strong, stable, or perhaps even growing in a positive direction. You may decide to try to increase this segment even further.
- Look at the areas of the wheel where you are not thriving. Is one of these calling to you for attention?
- Select an area from your completed wheel that you'd like to improve. Select the one that you feel ready to take action on. Take the time to think about how you might begin to change the situation by taking one small action-step at a time.

If, for example, you decide to focus on **Health**, and you decide that regular exercise will allow you to increase your current score, think about the next actions or steps you will take to make that happen.

- If, for example, your current score is 3, and you decide to try to move to a score of 5, think about all the things you can do to move your score in a positive direction.
- Every time you think of a positive action, write it down until you have recorded a possible 'to do' list.

One of the points on your list might be where you decide that you should include regular exercise into your daily routine.

You might say, *"I will start walking for a set distance/time every day"*.

Next ask yourself, *"What else can I do?"*

Your response might be, *"I will increase the distance I walk by 500 steps the next day"*.

Next, ask yourself, *"What else can I do?"*

You might decide that, *"I will increase the distance I walk the next day by a further 500 steps"*.

Then ask yourself, *"What else can I do to move towards a healthier/fitter version of me?"*

You might decide that, *"I will get myself a walking or accountability partner to encourage me to stick to my plan"*.

Finally, you might decide that walking six days per week for thirty to forty minutes each day will improve your health and fitness. If that is your decision, write your goal using positive and explicit language. Make sure your goal is **S.M.A.R.T.**

S – specific. What is the goal?

M –measurable. How will you measure your daily progress towards the goal?

A – achievable. Is it within your capability?

R – relevant. Does it help you make positive change and progress in your own life?

T – time-bound. Does it tell you when, and for how long, you will work on it each day?

Once you have assessed your goal, write it in the **present tense**, for example:

> ***By*** *June 1,* ***I am*** *walking 5 kilometres per day, 6 times per week,* ***so that*** *I am improving my heart health, my stamina, and my general fitness and well-being.*

You may decide to work on one segment of the wheel at a time. You may decide that you can work on several segments concurrently. Whatever you decide, display your wheel where you can see it. If you have the confidence to do so, share your plans, and possibly even your wheel, with your partner or a close friend. Your partner or friend may become your biggest cheerleader and accountability buddy. Regardless of whether you share your goal or not, the Wheel of Life can be a strong visual reminder of the area/areas on which you are focusing to progress your life in a more positive direction.

I sometimes think how useful this tool would have been when I began to study for my teaching degree in 1990 during a financial recession. With my decision to begin study, my life became extremely busy, even busier than before. Our children were then aged 14, 9, 7, 6 and 3. Interest rates were on the rise. They rose every month! Money was tight, and I was stretched in so many directions.

My study was stimulating and, at the same time, really challenging. Most often, it wasn't the work itself that caused the challenge, it was 'the juggle'. There were so many deadlines to meet, apart from those that came with running a really busy household. I'd set my alarm for 5.00am each day, and work on my assignments while I had an opportunity to study in a quiet house. I'd feed and organise my children, and get them off the school, to kinder, or to my sister or friend who were minding our youngest, so that I could attend lectures and tutorials.

University life offered me so much learning, and a chance to engage my mind and heart in something I was passionate about. It was a place where I was learning and growing. It was something that was just for me. It was the opportunity to finally begin the course I would have started when I was eighteen years old, had my life not taken a turn in a very different direction.

The pace of life in those days was extremely challenging. I didn't spend much time socialising with the other students at university. Instead, I felt as though I raced everywhere. I raced to class. I raced home to get the washing off the line. I raced to parent/teacher interviews, and to kinder and school events. I was heavily involved in my children's primary school Parents Association and School Council. I attended children's sports, and drove our kids to all the associated football and cricket training, and to their matches. I drove to playdates for the little ones, and to social catch ups and outings for our teenage son. We also had a fairly busy social life where we spent a lot of time enjoying our family and friends.

The wheels and tyres, on which I was trying so desperately to navigate my life, needed some attention. The tyres were set to different rates of pressure, the wheel rims were scuffed and dented. I didn't stop to notice. I didn't realise. I just kept forging ahead. Pushing, always pushing, towards my next deadline. If I'd had access to the Wheel of Life tool in those busy days, I'm sure my 33-year-old self would have been able to clearly see that several segments of the wheel were really out of balance, and that this was causing long term stress and pressure in my life. By not taking notice and care of my 'wheels' and 'tyres', I was not giving myself the best opportunity to thrive in the fast-paced world in which I lived.

Thinking back to this time in my life, I feel that I would have scored the segments of the wheel in the following way:

Health – 4
Family – 7
Relationships – 6
Social Life – 7
Attitude – 5
Career – 3
Finance – 4
Personal Growth – 2

Here is a visual representation of what my wheel would have looked like.

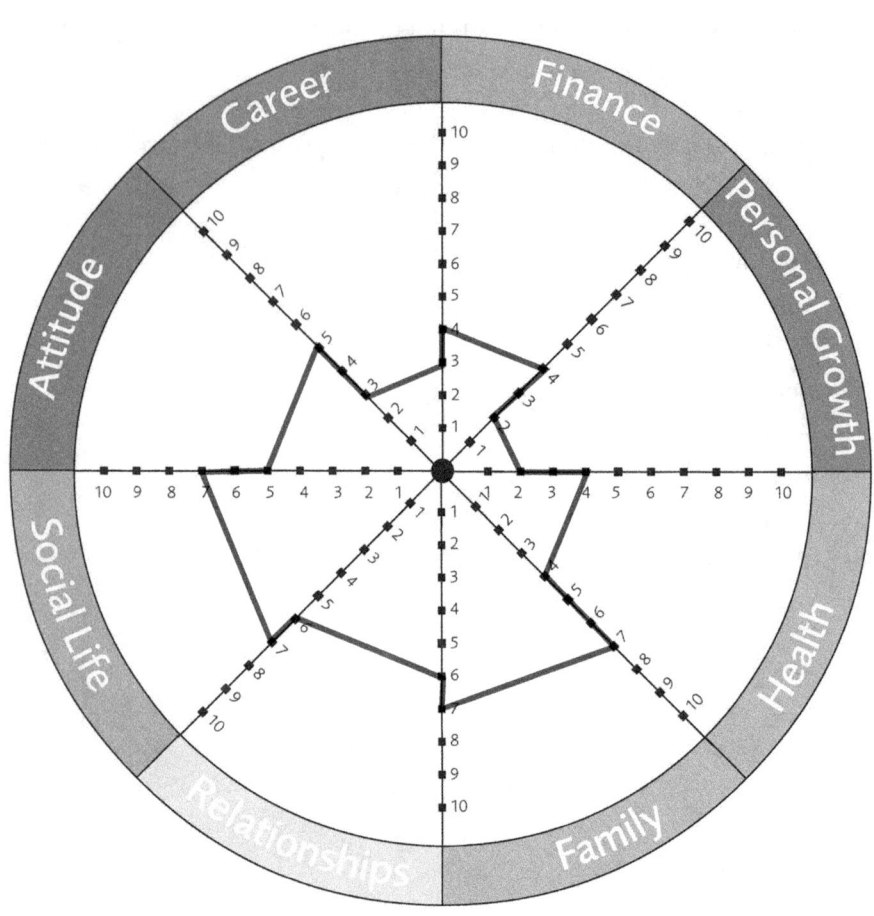

For the next six years I worked part-time, I studied full-time, and I parented full-time. I rode the highs, and the lows, of being a daughter, a partner, a mother, a sister, and a friend. There were many moments and situations that would have caused the segments of my wheel to rise and fall.

Looking back at this time in my life, I realise that the biggest problem I had was that I wasn't aware enough of the need for regular self-care and reflection. Without these two things, I believe that healthy self-leadership is impossible. I wasn't being a conscious leader of myself. I wasn't totally seated in the driver's seat of my own life. I was hurtling along, doing the best I could, but I was doing it all without a map. I needed a self-leadership map to help me guide and plan the steps ahead.

Since learning about the Wheel of Life, and other useful tracking tools, my life has changed immeasurably. Did it change because I learned and used the tools? Or did it change because I used them in conjunction with my self-leadership map? Basically, my results have changed because I took ACTION. I worried less. I tried hard to catch myself whenever I became aware that I was falling into the trap of wishing, procrastinating, and waiting for everything to be perfect. Perfectionism can be a truly dangerous trap to fall into, and it is an even more dangerous place to dwell for anything longer than just a few reflective moments.

Psychology Today tells us that, "*Perfectionism is a trait that makes life an endless report card on accomplishments or looks. When healthy, it can be self-motivating and drive you to overcome adversity and achieve success. When unhealthy, it can be a fast and enduring track to unhappiness. What makes extreme perfectionism so toxic is that while those in its grip desire success, they are most focused on avoiding failure, resulting in a negative orientation. They don't believe in unconditional love, expecting others' affection and approval to be dependent on a flawless performance.*"

I have often searched for perfection rather than for the next logical, incremental step along the way towards anything I wanted, or needed, to achieve in my life. If I didn't believe I could be perfect then often, I'd prefer not to try at all. Far too often in my life, I have let fear rule both my head and my heart.

One classic example of my fear/perfectionism occurred during my studies for my education degree. After a long and challenging five years of study, I was facing my final semester. I was excited! I was nearing the end of my long journey as a mature age student. Most students completed their degree within a four-year timeframe. I was slower because I began part-time, and because of other moments of procrastination and indecision that, I alone, had created.

There were two units of study in my course load that I needed to undertake before the academic component of my course was complete. The first was a unit entitled Mathematics Education, the second, Music Education. I told myself many stories about not being good at Maths. I told myself that it would be embarrassing if I couldn't complete the tasks and actually had to ask someone for help.

There she was again, my inner critic/ego telling me that I should be able to breeze through the course, and the associated assessment tasks, without having to show that I didn't understand, or that I needed support. She told me not to bother. She said to me time and time again, "If you can't do the Maths then you just can't teach!" She also said, "You've wasted so much time because you can't do the Maths, and without Maths, you can't be a primary school teacher".

My self-confidence was low. I was floundering and teetering on the edge of despair. I spent several weeks thinking about deferring the subject while I figured out what to do. I knew that this was a ridiculous idea but, once again, my fear drove me into panic and I was on the verge of possibly throwing it all away. When I finally let go of my panic and fear, I convinced myself that I would attend the first lecture and tutorial, and see how I progressed. Needless to say, this was a far wiser decision than running away without even trying.

I stuck at the subject and completed it. I received a credit as a grade for my work. I was satisfied and proud of what I had achieved. This is one example of not wanting to face my fears, or show up as a person who didn't know how to do something. There I was allowing my fear to drive me to consider 'throwing the baby out with the bathwater'!

If I was concerned in that final semester about having to study Maths Education, I was absolutely terrified at the thought of having to attend Music Education. I had heard many stories on campus about the Music Education tutor. She had a reputation for insisting that each student sing solo in her class. I will be the first to admit that singing is not my strong suit, and I really did not want to be asked to showcase my lack of singing talent in front of my fellow students or, more particularly, in front of the tutor!

Week after week, I headed to the music room with my heart in my mouth. Was today the day that I would be asked? I didn't know for sure. I lived through every class trying not to draw any attention to myself. I spent each class trying to make myself appear small and unnoticeable. At the conclusion of each lesson, I left the room feeling relieved that I had escaped yet again.

One day, during a class, the tutor announced that all students would be required to complete a practical performance as part of their final assessment. I froze. My heart raced as I listened attentively to the requirements of the task. To my utter amazement, the task did not require any student to sing solo. I couldn't believe my luck. I had dodged a bullet!

I was smiling inwardly as the tutor went on to explain the task we were required to complete. No, the task did not involve singing. It involved playing the recorder with a partner and then solo. 'How hard could it be?' I thought somewhat smugly to myself. I made arrangements with a friend from the course to play together for our duo performance. We selected a piece from the music book we were required to use. May I state here that the book was one used by primary school students aged approximately eight-years-old! We agreed that we would practise separately and then come together to ensure we were going to put in a passable performance on assessment day. I knew that I had time to prepare during the two-week semester break.

Much to the horror of my children, I took my recorder on holiday with us to Byron Bay. I diligently practised the piece I was to play with my partner at the upcoming assessment. I also practised the piece I was to perform solo. My children groaned every time the recorder came out of my bag. I thought I was improving, I'm not at all certain that they felt the same way!

The day of the assessment finally arrived, and my friend and I entered the music studio. We were a little nervous but overall, we were coping quite well. We played the piece together. Nobody died! There were no lightning bolts from the heavens. Were we extraordinary? No, I don't believe so. Did we put in a passable performance? Yes, it appeared that we had.

My friend was asked to wait outside and then it was my turn to perform. I sat at a piano stool with my music book resting upon the piano stand. I was nervous. I could feel the butterflies in my stomach. The tutor was seated at a small table that was positioned behind me at the back of the room. All of a sudden she said, "Commence". I began to play the simple little tune that I had selected. It didn't sound great. My recorder was squeaky. I was struggling. I was lost in the panic and embarrassment of knowing that things didn't sound as they should. I just kept battling my way through my performance hoping that very soon it would end.

The more overwhelmed and embarrassed I became, the worse the noise from my instrument sounded. All of a sudden I heard footsteps. My tutor walked across the room towards me. She placed her hand on my shoulder and said, "Sue, put the recorder down. Go back to the start of the book and find something you CAN play and start again." I thought I'd die of embarrassment at that point. As I shuffled the pages back towards the start of my book to find some simpler tunes, she had one last comment for me. She said, "By the way, if you use your thumb to completely cover the hole on the underside of the recorder, it will sound a whole lot better." Somehow through teary eyes, I made it to the end of the piece and left the room mortified. It had been a truly uncomfortable experience.

It is human nature to want to avoid many of the new, challenging or uncomfortable experiences that life inevitably throws at us. Perfectionism, in my case, is a convenient excuse to stay stuck, to spin my wheels, and to go absolutely nowhere. I have learned several things about new experiences:

- Sometimes, they are unavoidable.
- Often, what we avoid will be repeated.
- They always teach us something new about ourselves.
- Humour, an open mind, and stepping up with courage are useful tools when faced with the unknown or the uncomfortable.

Sometimes, where possible, when facing a new experience or avoiding one because I find myself using the perfectionism excuse, I go back to my belief statements and remind myself of some of my key messages. In situations such as the Music exam and the Maths subject, the following statements would have been useful:

- I am strong
- I am capable
- I am resilient
- I adapt to change and learn new things
- I AM ENOUGH

My life has become fuller, richer and calmer because I have made a plan, and because I have my self-leadership map to guide me. I hold myself accountable for my decisions and for my results. From time to time, when I feel stuck, uncertain or in need of a gentle but honest push, I check in with a coach or mentor. I cannot overstate the power of working with a coach or mentor. They are most often the people who encourage us to look beyond the stories we tell ourselves. They encourage us to take action towards living the life of our dreams. It has become one of my strongest beliefs that a 'healthy life' is one where we strive for balance and growth, rather than perfection or an all or nothing approach.

At this point in my story, I would like to acknowledge one of my coaches who first shared with me her wisdom and coaching tools, around regular planning and checking in. Shannah Kennedy, whom I have mentioned previously, and with whom I have had the privilege of working, taught me about the benefits of 'seasonal' planning and reflection. Shannah said that planning in seasons provides a person with a practical approach, and a timeframe for making plans, setting goals, and measuring outcomes and success. A period of three months is one quarter of a year. It is one season of the year. This amount of time provides you with a manageable number of weeks/months in which to enact part of your plan, achieve success, reflect on your progress, and plan again.

With Shannah's approach in mind, I decided that I would incorporate the use of The Wheel of Life into my seasonal planning. By using the wheel at the beginning of each season, I give myself a strong visual reminder of the progress I have made, and of the segments of the wheel (my life) that require a boost and, therefore, my focus and attention. This tool supports me in achieving healthy balance and perspective in my life.

In my search for effective approaches, tools and methods to manage myself, as I strived to fulfil my mission and live my dreams, I realised that following formula is a useful one to add to my self-leadership map:

Self-Leadership Map Signpost No:2
The Wheel of Life tool used once each season = a highly effective reality check on your life balance, personal growth and progress.

A Great Coaching Questions About Balance
What does balance look like for you?
Can you remember a time, and an area in your life, when you were in balance?
Create a mental picture of that time. What were you doing? How were you acting?
What attitudes, skills and actions could you apply from that time in your life to your life/situation now?

A Piece of Wisdom from Positive Psychology
This piece of wisdom from Positive Psychology elegantly explains the importance of striving to achieve balance in our lives if we are to experience high levels of wellbeing. It is my strong belief that The Wheel of Life is a wonderful visual tool/reminder to track our progress towards achieving this balance. While some areas receive all of your attention, others get none. Perhaps your career is on track, but you no longer have time for your family and friends, or your work is unfulfilling, and you are not growing or learning. You are not alone. Harmony in life – relationships, career, health, spirituality, finances, and beyond – is hard to achieve and seemingly impossible to maintain. Achieving a balanced existence is essential. After all, your mental wellbeing is underpinned by finding high levels of meaning within your daily tasks and activities. If the many aspects of your being find balance, then life satisfaction, the fulfilment of basic psychological needs, and contentment usually follow. (Eakman, 2016)

Chapter Four
Treasure Hunt Your Strengths

Turn Up the Volume

"The meaning of life is to find your gift.
The purpose of life is to give it away."

Pablo Picasso

Why is it that we find it so much easier to identify the strengths, talents and wonderful attributes of other people, than we do to confidently name and speak about our own? Strengths are part of the human condition, and they help to make up our personalities. They make us who we are. I first learned about strengths when studying for the 'Certificate in Positive Psychology' in 2016.

A survey designed by Christopher Petersen and Professor Martin Seligman is helpful in the identification of human strengths. The **VIA Inventory of Strengths**, formerly known as the 'Values in Action Inventory', is a psychological assessment measure designed to identify an individual's profile of character strengths. This survey asks a number of questions of participants. These questions help to identify people's strengths, and to rank them in order from 1 to 24. These strengths can also be grouped into clusters of virtues – Wisdom and Knowledge, Courage, Humanity, Justice, Temperance, and Transcendence.

There is a great deal of research that supports the notion that, when people work from their strengths, their learning, growth and progress develops, and is consolidated far more quickly than when they are encouraged to work from areas of challenge, deficit and weakness. When we work from a strengths basis, our motivation, confidence and willingness to try is greatly increased. We experience positive emotions related to consistent effort when working towards a change in our behaviour, habits or lifestyle, so we are more likely to stay focused on the change/growth process. In other words, the more often we experience 'success', positive challenge, or 'ease' during the learning process, the more likely we are to consolidate a new behaviour, skill or practice. This new behaviour will become part of our repertoire of skills that support us in developing strong self-leadership, and a more positive and fulfilling life.

When I elected to study for the Certificate in Positive Psychology, I was required to spend the first five days of the course as an 'on campus' student at the prestigious Geelong Grammar School in Victoria. I remember getting ready to leave my family and embark on this adventure. One part of me was excited, ready to learn new things and to meet new people. Another part of me, the part where my nagging inner critic lives, was less sure, less confident, perhaps even a little shy. I didn't know a single person who had enrolled in the course. With this in mind, I packed everything I thought I needed to 'look right' and to 'be right'. This was typical of me; outwardly confident and friendly but, at the same time, squashing down the more negative questions I often had about my self-worth, and my professional knowledge and experience.

What was it that made me so concerned about consistently 'showing up' as a confident and knowledgeable woman, who was always in control? Upon reflection, I realise that there is a large part of me that truly wants to be accepted by others. I also want to feel knowledgeable, confident, in control, and that I have something of value to add to any situation. Perhaps these feelings stem from how I felt as a much younger woman. I still often thought of myself as a pregnant teenager who was undereducated, yet clever and, in so many ways, very, very different from her peers. It is so easy to see how we can allow our past experiences to colour and shape who we are, and how we show up in the world.

As usual, it didn't take me all that long to connect with others at Geelong Grammar, and to absolutely thrive on the learning content and the experiences which immersed me in this new and exciting environment. The thinking and behaviours described in Positive Psychology were just perfect for me. Positive Psychology is about humanity, emotions, presence, action, accomplishment, happiness, and health. Its basic premise is that we do not need 'fixing'! Ultimately, each of us can work from our strengths, experience happiness, and grow and flourish as human beings.

> *"The good life is using your signature strengths every day to produce authentic happiness and abundant gratification."*
>
> Martin Seligman

You may be interested to know what my top five character strengths are. I have taken the VIA survey a number of times in the past nine years as the circumstances of my life have shifted and changed. It is interesting to note that four of my five top strengths have always been present in the list although, occasionally, they have changed in ranking order. I think this change in order may have something to do with how I am experiencing life at the time I take the test. I have also noted that sometimes the fifth strength will drop from the list to be replaced by another. Interestingly, the same two strengths are the ones that appear to alternate in my top five.

My top five strengths in order as I write this book are:

> **Love**
> **Kindness**
> **Social Intelligence**
> **Perspective**
> **Gratitude**

Sometimes when re-taking the test, **Gratitude** drops out of my top five and is replaced by **Appreciation of Beauty and Excellence**.

I remember the first time I took the survey, I was so keen to view the results very much from the standpoint of my work as a primary school principal. I was desperate to see where the character strength of **Leadership** would show up in my list. To my horror, Leadership was ranked at number twelve! I asked myself, "How can I lead a team of teachers, and an entire school community, if leadership is not showing up anywhere near my top five?" I was greatly relieved when it was explained to me that we can lead ourselves, and lead others, through employing our top strengths. I now know that I lead myself and others through Love, Kindness, Social Intelligence, Perspective, Gratitude and Appreciation of Beauty and Excellence. If you work with a team, it is a brilliant and worthwhile exercise to learn about the top strengths of all team members.

In 2018, when I eventually became capable of leading myself out of my burnout, I quickly realised that the best way to lead myself was through my top strengths of **Love, Kindness,** and **Gratitude**.

Leading myself with **Love** meant that I made sure I tried every day to take the time to honour the extraordinary human being I know deep in my heart that I am. I made sure that I took the time to:

- Wake up gently.
- Stretch my body as I arose from bed.
- Smile and say thank you as I began my day.
- Breathe deeply – three deep cleansing breaths.
- Make my bed so that when I returned to rest at night, I had a beautiful place to relax, unwind and sleep.

I made sure that I **loved** myself enough to:

- Notice the early morning beauty of nature, whether that be a bird song, a sunrise, or a deep, cold frost. I made sure to practise gratitude for these amazing feats of nature.

- Repeat my belief statements with a smile and conviction in front of my bathroom mirror – *I am strong, I am beautiful, I am confident, I am capable, I am resilient, I can l adapt to change and learn new things, I treat myself with respect, care and kindness, I treat others with kindness and respect, I am a communicator, I am a connector, I am a coach, I learn and grow every day, I am ENOUGH!*
- Walk each morning before work. My walks are always done without listening to anything on my phone – a conversation, a podcast or even music. Walking is my form of meditation where I practise mindfulness to help set me up with a positive mindset to begin my day.
- Enjoy that first sip of coffee as I made my way to school, or on the weekends to sit and enjoy a coffee with my husband and friends at a local café.
- Drink at least eight glasses of water each day to keep my body hydrated, ready to meet the joys and challenges of the day ahead.
- Celebrate in small ways the fact that I was still alive, healthy again, and engaging in life.

Leading myself with **Kindness** meant that I always tried to:

- Remember who I was when dealing with staff, students, parents, family, and friends.
- Take three deep breaths before embarking on challenging conversations, meetings, presentations, or tasks.
- Take breaks for water, movement, time away from my computer or phone screen, and for stretching my body.

Leading myself with **Gratitude** meant that I always tried to:

- Start and end my day with the practice of gratitude, where I thought about and wrote about the things for which I was grateful on that day. I wrote about the small improvements I had made in becoming well and strong again.
- I said 'thank you' often.
- I made real attempts to smile when engaging with others. This had always been my way of meeting, greeting and approaching others, but during this time of real struggle and low confidence, it became something I needed to remind myself of, and something I had to push to remember to do.

These behaviours have become habits that have helped me ensure that my wellbeing is always front of mind.

The character strengths I have mentioned here are only one part of the set of attributes that make me the unique and wonderful person I know I am. I have many other skills, interests, talents, and passions that also contribute to making me uniquely 'me'.

Whether or not you feel comfortable enough to acknowledge that you, too, are a gifted, unique, and beautiful person, I want to emphasise that you absolutely are. I strongly urge you to take the time to go on a 'treasure hunt' in your own life, by answering the following questions:

- **What are my interests?**
- **What are my hobbies?**
- **What are my talents and skills?**
- **What are the things I am good at?**
- **What am I doing when I shine?**

When I answered these questions, I came up with these answers.

- **What are my interests?**
  My interests include fashion, interior design, gardens and indoor plants, cooking, reading, walking in nature, spending time at the beach, travel, personal growth and development.

- **What are my hobbies?**
  My hobbies include cooking, writing, caring for my indoor plants and our herb garden, walking our dog, finding and collecting beautiful beach shells, exploring different suburbs and towns.

- **What are my talents and skills, the things I am good at?**
  I am good at speaking, writing, teaching, coaching and connecting with people, making delicious meals, creating spaces that are fragrant, beautiful, orderly and calm.

- **What am I doing when I shine?**
  I shine when I am using my gift of communicating with others, both personally and in both small and large groups. When I speak about my passions, my interests, and my areas of expertise, I sense that I can engage both the individual and the room. I shine when I have the opportunity to engage and connect with others. Whether speaking, writing, coaching, teaching, or socialising, I shine when I communicate.

I can think of many times in my life when I allowed my impressions of myself, and the opinions of others, to make me feel that I was not quite as bright and shiny as I should be. I have let my nagging inner critic tell me that I wasn't a match for the people I was spending time with. This feeling occurred often in my early twenties when we regularly socialised with a group of people who had attended some of Melbourne's most prestigious schools, and were either studying for 'important' degrees at university, or had begun important careers in law, medicine or business. They came from wealthy families who lived in the leafy suburbs of Melbourne. I knew I was attractive. I knew I was intelligent, but I always allowed my inner voice to tell me that I was actually quite ordinary among these people. It is important to mention that it was not them who made me feel this way. I was doing a brilliant job of that all by myself!

As I have mentioned previously, another aspect of my personality that hasn't always allowed me to use and play to my strengths, is my strong need and drive to be seen as 'good and perfect'. Throughout my childhood, in my teenage years, and sometimes as a grown woman, I have felt the pressure to show myself as knowledgeable, highly accomplished, appropriate, certain, and always in control.

I guess somewhere deep inside me, I always had an innate drive to be seen as 'the best'. I am not certain what made me feel this way but I guess it has something to do with my need for approval – approval from my parents, my teachers, my siblings, and my peers. I believe that wanting to be seen as 'the best' made me feel safe from scrutiny, ridicule, and any form of punishment. I was looking for security and safety. I was becoming someone who needed to make sure she always 'coloured within the lines'. I would go so far as to describe myself as a person who often plays it safe. I am not by nature a risk taker.

I have several strong, early memories of childhood events that made me extremely keen to either stand out as 'bright and shiny', or play it safe to avoid unwanted attention. In my first two years of schooling at a crowded Catholic primary school, where the classes sometimes exceeded fifty students, my drive was always to be a very well-behaved, compliant student, a 'good girl', in order to avoid any unnecessary negative attention from my less than warm and encouraging teacher. When I felt certain that I could complete the task successfully, or answer the question correctly, I did just that. When I was correct, and when my efforts were satisfactory, I felt safe. I knew that there would be no verbal reprimand nor punishment for my efforts.

I believe that, to a large degree, I wanted security and safety. In a time when corporal punishment was 'commonplace' in schools, I lived and worked with an underlying fear of having to witness children being severely reprimanded and punished, or to possibly experience this type of treatment myself. I want to make it clear that this was not how we lived in our family home. I didn't live in fear of punishment there. I always knew, however, that I was expected to 'behave'. And behave I did, because everywhere I went it reinforced to me that children who did what they were told didn't have to face the displeasure or disapproval of the 'grown ups'. I always played for safety. I didn't want to make any mistakes because I did not want to experience the possible consequences.

My memories are so strong of a time when I was about seven years old, my two sisters and I stayed at the home of my aunt for the weekend while my parents were away. I remember playing a game of 'school' where, of course, I was the teacher. It was a sunny afternoon in my aunt's garden, and I used a grey lead pencil to carefully and neatly write on her very clean garage wall the Math equations and spelling words I was teaching to my imaginary students. To this day, I don't even need to close my eyes to see that wall and my handwriting that adorned it.

$$1+1=2$$
$$2+2=4$$
$$3+3=6$$

d o g
c a t
m u m
d a d
g i r l
b o y

I'm sure I didn't think I was doing anything wrong but, if I had, surely I would have 'taught my lesson' on a far more discreet, less obvious, or even an imaginary wall! What I remember was my shock at the sting of my aunt's words when she expressed her displeasure at what I had done. I remember feeling embarrassed, nervous, and experiencing a really strong desire to go home. Was this a 'defining moment' that helped shape my need to play for safety? I'm not sure. I just know that if there was a chance of 'getting into trouble', I didn't want to be part of it.

As I grew into my teenage years and beyond, I was most often, but not always, a rule follower rather than a rule breaker. At the same time, I cannot deny that I didn't enjoy the spotlight, the opportunity to excel and to shine. If there was an opportunity to showcase something I knew I could do very well, I was always one of the first to volunteer.

At school, if the task involved using my excellent memory, spelling a difficult word, writing an essay, sharing my general knowledge, or giving an opinion and backing it up with supporting evidence, I was always there, wanting to be seen and heard. I loved the spotlight when I was confident, and certain that I was correct. The areas where I was far less confident were things such singing, dancing, or acting in a solo capacity. I was far less confident when asked to do any of these activities, and I would always hope like crazy that I would never be asked, or expected, to perform solo in the area of the performing arts!

When I became a primary school principal thirteen years ago, I was often overwhelmed by the strong feelings of not being quite good enough. These feelings often arose when I attended meetings with other principals from our region. I would attend a meeting, and there, sitting on my shoulder, would be my nagging inner critic. She'd often show up just in time to chip away at my self-confidence by telling me that I may look like a principal, and act like a principal, but if anyone ever bothered to scratch the surface of my facade, they would quickly realise that I knew very little, and that I really wasn't worthy of the role.

I allowed my inner critic to take me to so many uncomfortable places of self-doubt and worry. I allowed her to get into my head, making comments that reminded me that I was a fraud! She reminded me that, if I wasn't very careful, someone would realise that it was a big mistake to have given me such an important role. I was doing an excellent job of 'overwhelm'. I now believe that it is often easier to 'sit in overwhelm' than it is to step out of my comfort zone and 'have a go', or to ask for help. It took me quite a while to realise that I was doing a job. Yes, it is an important job. I was doing it well and, so long as I wasn't frightened to ask questions and seek support from the principals I admired, trusted and respected, I was learning, growing and evolving into the principal and leader I needed to be.

What I find interesting is the two sides of the one coin that are really obvious in my personality. I wanted to stand out when I was confident and playing to my strengths, and I wanted to hide under a rock when called on to take any sort of an uncomfortable risk. I suppose this is not all that unusual. From a very young age, I have always been responsible for at least one person other than myself. As an adult, I definitely prefer security over 'going out on a limb'. I go out on a limb when I am reasonably confident that I can do well. When I feel there is a big risk involved, particularly, a financial risk, I find myself drawn to 'playing it safe'.

What was it inside me that made me feel as though I wasn't good enough? As I look back, I can see that, in my younger days, it was a lack of maturity and experience that made me feel that way. Throughout my early life, I didn't have many people who told me often enough that I was doing a good job. It wasn't that I was criticised, or told I was doing poorly. It seems to me now that there was just a lack of positive and constructive encouragement and feedback. Perhaps this was a sign of the times, perhaps this was the way my parents were parented during their childhoods.

Later on in life, I realised that my inner critic was actually my ego at work. My ego wanted me to stay exactly as I was. The ego is not a fan of evolution and growth. My ego preferred for me to stay stuck! Eventually I realised that, whenever I felt unsure and vulnerable, I needed to remember to look at the many treasures, gifts and talents that were mine to show and to share with the world. I needed to remember all of the good, positive, and life-giving qualities I possessed. In those times of doubt, I really needed my most important belief statement – I AM ENOUGH! You may remember from earlier in my book that these words are the final ones in my list of self-belief statements. These are now the words that have become so important to me that I say them to myself every morning, and these are words that I now believe to be true. These are the words I use to open up confidence and trust in myself, so that I can continue to learn and grow.

I can hear you thinking:

- *'If you think you are enough, does that mean you are completely satisfied with your performance in every facet of your life?'*
- *'Does that mean that you believe that you will never have to strive for any goal, any achievement, or any improvement ever again?'*

My answer is simple, absolutely not! I strive daily in almost every area of my life:

- I strive to increase my health and fitness.
- I strive for an evolution into the next phase of my career.
- I strive to grow and strengthen my financial position.
- I strive to show up in the world as a kind, loving, and interested person.
- I strive to learn more about how to evolve as a high functioning human being.

I believe it is important that I approach all of this striving from a different place. Instead of approaching it from a place of fear and lack, I now come from a place of curiosity, appreciation, and gratitude. I fully appreciate the treasures I have been gifted with in my life – my talents, my skills, my abilities, my physical and mental health.

I know that:

1. I am worthy of living my life on this planet.
2. I know I can improve and refine every aspect of my life through action, consistent effort, and practice.
3. I know how to appreciate, and use, my character strengths and my talents.

Recently, I thought that I would step into courage, and attend an open-mic storytelling event that is held monthly at a suburban Melbourne hotel. I had followed the founder of the event for several months on social media, and I thought speaking at an event such as this would give me a taste of speaking to an audience I didn't know. I was, of course, quite comfortable speaking to known groups – such as staff, parents, principal colleagues, and groups of middle leaders within the education system in which I worked.

Many colleagues, who know me well, would probably say that speaking on my subject was one of the places I appeared happiest, and where I shone. I agree with their appraisal. I was curious as to how I would fare when the audience was completely unknown. It is one of my long-held dreams to become a speaker, perhaps one day as even a keynote speaker, who connects with groups on a broader level than I do presently. I really liked the theme of the session I thought I might attend. It was entitled 'Metamorphosis Moments'. I thought it had my name written all over it. So I purchased a ticket, and emailed the host to say that I would like to speak at the event.

During the weeks leading up to the event, I was extremely busy and did not have much free time. I had chosen the story I was going to tell. Each time I thought about it, I couldn't quite decide exactly how to end it, given that I had ten precious minutes in which to speak. As I have previously mentioned, sometimes, when I'm stepping out of my comfort zone, my inner critic turns up to cause some chaos and some doubt. I found that I was constantly telling myself that the story was perhaps too precious, and too private to share. I found myself considering whether I even had the right to tell my story in this type of forum. My doubtful self-won the battle in my head, and I emailed the host to say that I'd attend the event, but that my story wasn't prepared sufficiently to share. She was understanding and kind. She said that if I changed my mind, I could still speak at the event.

The night arrived, and I drove myself to the hotel where the event was to take place. I parked my car in the dark street, went into the hotel, ordered myself a glass of wine, and headed upstairs where I met the host. She was a warm, friendly, and encouraging woman who immediately made me feel welcome. I sat down and soon began chatting with several other women as they arrived. I have never found small talk, and being friendly and open, a challenge. Soon it was time for the speakers to commence, I nestled into my seat, sipped my wine, and relaxed.

The host warmly welcomed all comers and explained that the storytelling event is a safe place for people to share their recollections and experiences. She said that it was customary for the host to tell the first story. She went on to explain that each speaker would have ten minutes in which to speak. She said that a timer would sound at the eight-minute mark, and then again at ten minutes. She went on to explain that if you hadn't finished speaking by eleven minutes, they would use a hook to drag you off the stage! She then explained that, at the end of each story, the audience was expected to offer warm, encouraging and generous applause. They were then asked to offer feedback to the speaker. Soon it was time for the guest story tellers to begin.

Two women told their stories, and were met with great encouragement and positivity for their efforts. Then, there was a lull. Who was going to speak next? One woman said she'd like to tell her story but did not, for some reason, want to be the third speaker! I'm not at all sure of her reasons for this, but the silence and the squirming in the seats was becoming a little awkward, so the host tried some gentle encouragement.

Before I knew it, my hand was in the air and I was being applauded as I walked to the stage. I stood in front of the microphone, and was met by a small sea of expectant faces, and so I began. I began to tell the story of the 17-year-old girl who, in her final year of schooling, found herself alone, frightened, and pregnant. I told the story of how I came to be in that situation. I told of the three months of sleepless nights that I lived through in the early days of my pregnancy. I outlined the fear, the dread, and the worry that I experienced as I thought about what I would, or could, do next. I spoke about the swirl of emotions I experienced, as each passing day made it abundantly clear to me that this new and terrifying experience was reality. I spoke of my shame at this happening to me at the tender age of seventeen. I spoke about the fact that I was alone. I explained that I had ended the relationship with the father of my baby just weeks before I realised the challenging situation I found myself in. I was not in love with him, and now, I was alone.

I felt my audience 'lean in' as I explained that every spare minute of my day was taken up with thinking about what I would, or could, do next. Every night I was consumed by sleeplessness, worry, fear, and dread. I continually asked myself how I was going to open my lips, and let the words "I'm pregnant" tumble from them. I just couldn't find a way. I wanted so desperately to tell my mother, but something always held me back. I didn't want to tell my father because I thought that I had really slipped from the standard I felt he expected of me. I didn't tell my sisters because they were fifteen and fourteen years old at the time, and I didn't see how they could possibly help. I didn't tell my closest girlfriends because I just couldn't say the words that would separate me from them by virtue of the fact that I was going to be a mother, and they were living their lives as 17-year-olds should.

They say that every compelling story should have at least one highpoint or climactic moment. In this life-shaping story, one of these moments came on a weeknight evening in our family home. I was in the kitchen with my mum, as she was preparing to serve a roast dinner. I still remember it like it was yesterday. She asked me what was wrong. I replied in what I assume was a typically 'teenagerish' way, "Nothing". My mother was persistent, and asked again. I offered the same response.

There was a moment's silence, and then what she said next blew me away! She looked at me and said, "You're pregnant aren't you?" My face fell, and she knew. Her hunch had been confirmed. It was as though the next part of this quite dramatic scene happened in slow motion. She put down the knife she was using to carve the roast, walked into our living room and said to my dad, "Sue and I are going for a drive. Will you please finish serving the dinner?" With that, we got into the car and drove to a local beach, and parked in the carpark.

As we began to talk, I cried and cried. My mother was wonderfully supportive. She listened as the many thoughts and emotions I had been holding onto for so long tumbled from my lips. My ideas were so mixed up. Some were irrational. I guess it showed just how young and scared I was. After talking with her for a really long time, I knew that I was going to have my baby, and I knew that my parents would support me. At no stage of the conversation did my mother try to pressure me in any way. I don't remember the drive home at all, I just remember going straight to bed and sleeping more soundly than I had in three months.

I awoke the following morning to my father standing in my bedroom. He was holding a cup of tea, with two pieces of toast and Vegemite. After he set them down, he bent down, gave me a hug and told me that it would be okay, and that he and my mother would be there to support me. I could hear my audience respond with little murmurs of approval when they heard this tender part of the story that involved me and Vegemite toast!

As I moved on with my story, I chronicled the nerve-wracking experience of going to my Catholic girl's school with my mother to inform them that I would not be returning for Term Two of the 1975 school year. I told the audience that I can remember very little of the experience, except for the fact that we entered the college through the front door. To my knowledge, nobody, certainly not a student, ever entered through the front door! I did recall the holy pictures, the darkish rooms, the arrangements of flowers, and the smell of furniture polish. As for the conversation and the massive disclosure that took place, I barely recall a word. The one thing that stood out for me was the offer from the principal for me to continue my studies, regardless of my situation. This offer was quickly declined by me, but I often reflect on the generous nature of it considering both the decade and the denomination of the school.

At this point in my story, the buzzer sounded giving me the warning that I had two minutes to complete the tale of my life changing, life shaping event. I rounded out my story by moving on to the climax, my ultimate 'Metamorphosis Moment'. I told the audience that I gave birth to my beautiful son on the day of the Year 12 English exam and that from that moment on, I was forever changed. Ready or not, I had emerged from the experience as a woman and a mother.

I completed recounting my story and was met by wonderfully warm and generous applause. I listened to the feedback supplied by the audience, and I felt brave, acknowledged, and satisfied. I had received the feedback I had been seeking. I knew that I could engage an audience of strangers in similar ways that I engaged those who knew me. I had stepped out of my comfort zone. I had played to my strengths. My passion for speaking and storytelling was confirmed. It became just so clear to me that stepping out of my comfort zone was where both the growth and the magic happens.

These are the gems I have found on my personal treasure hunt to grow, enjoy, and enrich my life. I am fully aware that, when I use these gifts and skills effectively, I place myself clearly in the driver's seat as I journey through life with purpose, and with a well-designed self-leadership map.

I encourage you to take the time to go on your own treasure hunt, and to answer the self-reflection questions I have included in this chapter. Take the time out to notice and appreciate just how unique and special you are.

I have listed the questions for you to consider, and I have included a table where you can record your answers.

- **What are my interests?**
- **What are my hobbies?**
- **What are my talents and skills?**
- **What are the things I am good at?**

Interests	Talents	Skills	Hobbies

Now that you have conducted what is hopefully an honest and generous self-inventory of your strengths, talents and abilities, I hope that you can move forward on your journey through life, more secure in the knowledge that you are worth the effort. You are your own best advocate and coach. Self-awareness and self-appreciation are some of the hallmarks of a highly evolved human being. When you work to develop these skills, two things happen:

- You become aware of and grateful for the unique strengths, abilities, and skills with which you have been gifted.
- You are better able to appreciate and celebrate the gifts and talents of others.

Above all, you come to realise that you are capable and worthy of designing and living your own brilliant life! I truly believe that playing from your strengths leads you along the path of growth and success. I realise that the following formula is a useful one to add to my self-leadership map:

Self-Leadership Map Signpost No:3

Strengths-based living = the formula for a happier, healthier, more confident you.

Great Coaching Questions About Strengths

Right off the top of your head, name three of your strengths.

Tell me about the situations that make you feel energised and excited.

When did you feel confident and accomplished?

What traits did you use in that situation?

A Piece of Wisdom from Positive Psychology

Our strengths lead us to positive emotions and relationships, greater vitality, and meaningful life activities. We flourish when we identify and flex our strengths. If we want to build up any of these strengths, we can learn to do so.

Chapter Five
Get Comfortable In Your Own Skin

Fall in Love with You

"A flower does not think of competing with the flower next to it. It just blooms."

Zen Shin

I have a strong feeling that some of you may struggle with the content when you read this chapter of my book. When I say "get comfortable in your own skin and fall in love with you", I believe that you may want to run a mile! You may want to put my book back on the shelf and shout, "Forget it! I'm not reading this. It just doesn't make sense."

Why is it that we struggle to find certain aspects of our bodies, personalities, minds, and hearts so difficult to notice, love, appreciate, and celebrate? Many of us are used to falling into, and relying upon, what I like to call the 'comparison trap'.

Throughout our lives, we are exposed to so many images of others. These images are often photoshopped, or have had 'golden, dreamy' filters applied to them before they are launched on social media platforms, and are used to bombard or seduce an often unaware and image hungry public. Is it any wonder that, in our social media driven, perfection driven, youth driven culture, we struggle to see how we can ever measure up? I believe it is important to mention at this point that each of us is unique. There never was, and there will never again, be anyone just like you. No-one has the same fingerprint as yours! No-one has exactly the same DNA as you. You are a walking miracle. You are a work of art. You are just so beautiful in your own unique way.

If this is truly the case, then how do we combat our own negative self-talk, and the constant chatter that goes on inside our heads, reminding us that we are not quite beautiful enough, smart enough, rich enough, or popular enough? How do we stop comparing ourselves with others? How do we change the conversations that we have with ourselves? How do we recognise and then, ultimately, decide that we are enough?

> *"To shine your brightest light is to be who you truly are."*
>
> Roy T. Bennett

As I write this chapter of my book, I am holidaying in Byron Bay. I have holidayed here for over twenty years, and many times I have caught myself falling into exactly this trap. A trip to the beach is all many of us need to fall down the rabbit hole of comparison, of not being slim enough, attractive enough, fit enough, young enough, and the list goes on. How is it that so many of us allow ourselves to fall into the trap of 'not enough'? I believe that comparison often brings about the potential for confirmation bias to occur. Confirmation bias is the tendency to search for, interpret, favour, and recall information in a way that confirms or supports one's prior beliefs or values. From this standpoint, if you believe that you are 'not enough', you will certainly find evidence to support your unresourceful view of yourself.

A chance for a promotion, a change of job or career, and the same voice often arises. Not skilled enough, not talented enough, not experienced enough. I held myself back for years in my efforts to develop and grow my career. I always told myself that there would be someone else who could do the job better than me. I also told myself that if I was successful in gaining the role or promotion, I would probably be found out by others as not as skilled, or capable, as they initially thought. I might just be thought of as a fraud!

In order to avoid this type of unhelpful behaviour, I believe it is important to answer these important and challenging questions:

- How do I fall in love with myself?
- How do I recognise and celebrate my own self-worth?

The answers appear to be just so tricky at first glance. We can easily allow ourselves to fall down the 'rabbit hole' of self-doubt and of 'not enough'! If you choose to spend your time scrolling through social media, absorbing the carefully curated images of others living 'golden lives', you will always come up feeling dissatisfied, slightly anxious, and very ordinary.

There is a saying that I strongly believe in. It is,

> *"What you focus on is what you notice."*

If you focus on looking for white BMWs, you will begin to see white BMWs everywhere you travel. If you focus on looking for people who never smile, you will find them too. If you focus on looking for something, either positive or negative in yourself, you will begin to notice it. It will show up everywhere to support your thoughts and your beliefs about yourself.

Positive attention is one way to fall in love with who we are. Other ways that add to, and support, positive attention are the practices of gratitude and appreciation. When I began to think about this idea several years ago, I designed a chart to use in an audit where I looked at every aspect of myself. I created the chart with headings that include the essential elements that make up the human person and their human experience. Then I asked myself, "What are the things I recognise, appreciate and celebrate as beautiful, valuable and worthwhile about myself?"

These are the headings I included in my chart:

- **Physical** – What do I appreciate about my body and its capabilities?
- **Spiritual** – What do I appreciate about my ability to connect with things of a higher order that are greater than me?

- **Intellectual** – What does my intelligence allow me to do well?
- **Social** – What do I enjoy and do well when engaging with others?
- **Creative** – How do I express and celebrate my creative self?

After deciding upon these headings, I placed them in a table, and then carefully considered myself and the things I liked and appreciated about myself in each category. As I thought of an attribute I appreciated about myself, I added it to my list under the appropriate column.

Let me show you an example of how I thought about the physical aspects of myself. When thinking about my body, I considered the way it looks, and the way it functions. For example, I love the way my lungs fill with air to keep me oxygenated and alive. I love the way my eyes sparkle and shine with happiness, and optimism, when I do something that supports the truest and highest version of myself. I have chosen to share with you the chart I completed about one year ago.

My completed chart:

Physical	Spiritual	Intellectual	Social	Creative
My expressive blue/green eyes.	My heart that is open to see the beauty and the good in other people and in the world.	My brain/mind that helps me to learn, to notice and to grow as an ever-evolving human being.	My ability to build rapport with a wide variety of people.	My ability to make spaces beautiful. My home and my office reflect my personal style, taste and creativity.
My legs that carry me on the journey of life.	My soul that is deeply connected to my heart. This is the spark of the divine in me.	My ability to listen to information and to retain it. My ability to absorb information and to often use it in creative ways.	My warmth and ease when connecting with others.	My ability to be confident in my sense of personal style. My style is professionally appropriate. It suits me and expresses who I am in my private life as well.
My hair is easy to style and usually looks good.	My ability to take myself to the quiet places in nature and within myself.	My ability to use words to speak and write so that I can powerfully communicate with others.	My ability to make people feel seen, heard, and appreciated.	My ability to cook beautiful food, most often without using recipe books.

GET COMFORTABLE IN YOUR OWN SKIN

My smile lets people know so much about who I am, and how I show up in the world as a welcoming, warm and open person.	My whole being that can enter into prayer and reflection – the part of me that connects easily with God and the universe.	My ability to speak. The ability to stand in my power with the confidence to deliver a heartfelt message to others.	My ability to instinctively know what is socially appropriate and required in most situations.	My ability to use my thoughts, words and ideas in creative ways to connect with and to inspire others.
My body has allowed me to carry and give birth to five beautiful babies. My body that functions so effectively, heals itself when it needs to, and carries me through life so that I am well almost all of the time.	The gift of wonder and awe that I access many times a day as I witness beauty in other people and in nature.	My ability to teach. My knowledge of how to model new concepts, to explain things in a variety of different ways in order to assist others to learn new content and skills.	My ability to make people feel special. My ability to openly tell them of the wonderful qualities I see in them.	My creativity allows me to think through ideas and situations, so that I come up with new and innovative ways to make the mundane tasks and duties of life more interesting and meaningful
My voice that allows me to speak, connect and communicate in powerful and effective ways.	My sixth sense that often allows me to see the synchronicity of life. I notice moments, connections and links that often serve me.	My ability to see links and make connections between things. My ability to use these to effectively teach and coach others.	My ability to remember people's names and to use them often. My awareness that people appreciate being remembered and called by their names.	My creativity allows me to imagine how projects will look, and how they will communicate my thoughts and ideas to others.

Completing a chart such as this can be a somewhat daunting task. We don't always find it easy to recognise and celebrate the positive aspects of ourselves.

My suggestions for engaging with this work include the following action steps:

- Find a notepad that you can keep handy.
- Write one heading from the chart on each page.
- On the first page, write the word **Physical**.
- *On this page, record anything you appreciate about your physical body and the way it works.*
- On the second page, write the word **Spiritual**.
- *On this page, record anything you appreciate about your emotions, feelings, inner self, your relationship with God, Spirit, a Higher Power, the Universe, yourself.*
- On the third page, write the word **Intellectual**.
- *On this page, record anything that you appreciate about your mind and its amazing ability to think, process, remember, plan, organise, and analyse, so that you can live your life.*
- On the fourth page write the word **Social**.
- *On this page, record anything you appreciate about your ability, skills and competence to meet and connect with other people in ways that allow each person to feel good about themselves in your presence.*
- On the fifth page write the word **Creative**.
- *On this page, record anything you appreciate about your ability to generate new ideas, use your ingenuity, connect ideas in new and interesting ways, make items or products, systems, spaces, and art works, that inspire and spark imagination and appreciation.*

Every time you think of another idea, record it on the appropriate page. If you have people in your life that you feel comfortable enough to ask, you may like to ask them what they notice about a particular aspect of you. Record their ideas too. Over a few days, write and adjust your list until you feel comfortable with it. Play with the wording until it sounds both authentic and positive in tone. When you feel fairly comfortable, you might like to complete the blank table that I have included here for your use.

Physical	Spiritual	Intellectual	Social	Creative

It is my sincere hope that, by engaging in this task, you will come to be more acutely aware of the many aspects of yourself that are worth celebrating. These aspects of you are the things you can use to enrich your own life, and to enrich your family, your community and, possibly, the world. These are the aspects of you that help you know how to lead yourself with confidence and positivity through life.

> **"How you love yourself is how you teach others to love you."**
> *Rupi Kaur*

Always remember that you are a unique work of art. It is only when you begin to recognise and celebrate your worth that other people will recognise and, often, marvel at your self-awareness and at your confidence. There is nothing more engaging and attractive than a person who consistently demonstrates that they are comfortable in their own skin. From this standpoint, I truly believe that this way of being makes it easier to face the world with confidence. This way of being helps you to actively participate in and enjoy your life, and all the opportunities that will come your way.

> **Remember that self-appreciation should form a key part of your self- leadership map.**

There have been many times in my life where I did not love myself enough. Often I did not love and appreciate myself, as I now understand I should. Most often these times occurred when I looked at myself through the lens of comparison. As a very young woman, I often compared my body to the bodies of other young women my age who had not born children. When I did this, I noticed I always came up feeling not quite as positive, bright and shiny as I knew, deep in my heart, that I should.

As an older woman, I am much more aware of my ageing than at any other time in my life, and I can sometimes allow myself to fall into negative and unresourceful ways of thinking. With the many hormonal changes that occur naturally within my body chemistry, I can easily allow myself to slip into the negative space of feeling dejected, flat, and without the vibrant spark that comes from viewing myself with respect, positivity, appreciation, and love. I recognise that I am at my best when I am making positive decisions, and taking positive actions towards my own health and happiness.

> *"I must emphasise that I believe I am totally responsible for the choices I make each and every day."*

So often these days, when I connect with other women – my sisters, my friends, and also with women much younger than me, who are often the parents in my school community – I hear stories of real struggle with self-image, self-confidence, and self-love. It is so easy to allow ourselves to feel this way, and I understand that the reasons for experiencing such emotions are many and varied. The reasons may include the following:

- Lack of time and financial resources, sometimes due to caring for young families and paying high rents or mortgages.

- Feeling as though their time is completely given to young children and their needs.
- Lack of support from partners, and other family members, who do not show interest or care about their hopes, ambitions, and dreams.
- A total focus on what is changing as they age – perhaps their skin has lost the dewy plumpness of youth, their body is softer, rounder and wider than it once was, they are experiencing the challenges of perimenopause or menopause.

I want to very clearly state that I believe that comparison is the thief of confidence. Without confidence, life is a real grind that is flat, colourless, and often a real struggle.

When I choose to reframe my negative thoughts, I take charge of my life and act with positivity and joy, I build real confidence. When I am full of confidence, it shines from me like a beacon, and the energetic field around me is magnetically attractive. I attract the people, connections, and opportunities I seek, that will often lead me in the positive direction of my dreams and goals. When I act from a place of positivity and confidence, other people notice.

Since I have begun to work towards developing a positive and proactive lifestyle, and way of being, my confidence has soared. I am much more inclined to grab opportunities with both hands that are presented to me, and say why not? I project myself forward with confidence knowing that, at the very least, I will learn and grow. I also tell myself that I may actually find new opportunities to pursue, and that I may make happen the things I really want in my life. Self-confidence and self-appreciation will always be positive guides as I follow my self-leadership map.

Self-Leadership Map Signpost No:4

Appreciation of all aspects of your unique self = a person who knows their worth, and lives with true confidence.

Great Coaching Questions About Self-Love

How do you currently love yourself?

Is there anything you do daily that inspires self-love, and makes you feel worthy, valuable, and important?

Describe your current self-care routine.

What actions do you take each day that build confidence, self-appreciation and love?

A Piece of Wisdom from Positive Psychology

As Jeffrey Borenstein, President of the Brain & Behavior Research Foundation, puts it: "Self-love is a state of appreciation for oneself that grows from actions that support our physical, psychological and spiritual growth. Self-love means having a high regard for your own well-being and happiness.

Chapter Six
Celebrate Imperfection

Threads of Gold

"Your cracks can become the most beautiful part of you."

Candice Kumai

CELEBRATE IMPERFECTION

There is not a person alive who has not, or will not, experience problems, confronting situations, or life challenging events during their lifetime. These inevitable events sometimes bring us to our knees. They may cause us to ask, "Who am I?" They may cause us to say, "Why am I going through this, and how will I ever feel safe and secure again?" Each day we live, we experience situations that may chip away at our self-confidence, our energy, our resilience, and our self-belief. Sometimes these situations can shake us to our very core. These events are the ones that challenge us in every way possible.

In my own experience, I have dealt with many issues and situations that have caused me to doubt myself. They have caused me to be so fearful that, for a time, I was frozen in a state of indecision and inaction. These life challenges leave scratches, chips, dents, fracture lines and, sometimes, actual breaks in our bodies, minds, hearts and souls. They sometimes cause us to wrestle with the question, "Now that this has happened, who am I?"

These challenges often make our shiny exteriors look less shiny, less attractive, less confident and more fragile. They sometimes make us feel completely broken. They are indeed the very experiences that make us vulnerable. Sometimes, we are broken down to such a degree that we need time, space and support to get back on the road, and to actually start living again. Each scratch, dent or crack eventually shapes us.

Significant challenges and events make us who we are. They reinforce our uniqueness. They add a certain patina, pathos, and wisdom to our hearts, minds, souls, and stories. When we are finally able to process, and then eventually embrace, these challenging events as part of our own unique story, we become stronger, more resilient and more beautiful than we were before. When we choose to embrace and learn from these moments, we grow. Growth is key. Growth keeps us from stagnating. Growth can be painful but it is what makes us truly interesting and beautiful. Growth eventually brings wisdom.

In Japanese culture, there is an ancient art form known as Kintsugi. It is the art of repairing broken pottery. It is known as 'golden joinery'. This ancient Japanese tradition calls for damaged or broken items to be treated with respect and care. They are not simply discarded or deemed useless. The chips, fractures and actual breaks in the pieces of pottery are repaired with gold, silver, or platinum. In this process, the damaged area is actually highlighted, strengthened and enhanced through the Kintsugi art form. This process of repair and restoration clearly supports, and highlights, my belief in the beauty of imperfection and vulnerability. It demonstrates that when we are eventually able to embrace our challenges, we can be put back together – not exactly as we were before but often richer, wiser, more human and more beautiful.

When we choose to reveal our scars to others, we take a risk in rendering ourselves vulnerable. But, when we do, we often also demonstrate the beauty of overcoming, of rising, and of growing through human struggle. Without realising, we often connect with, and inspire, others in ways we did not imagine possible. When we choose to look at ourselves and others with respect, care and appreciation, we often realise that what cracks us open, often makes us more beautiful, interesting, resilient, unique and wise.

> *"Oh my darling it's true.*
>
> *Beautiful things have dents and scratches too."*
>
> *Matt Hogan*

Many years ago, one of my closest friends was diagnosed with breast cancer. She was a beautiful, vibrant woman with a young family. We had been friends since we were sixteen years old. One day her husband called me with the devastating news that she was in hospital, and would undergo a radical mastectomy the following morning. I was shocked, deeply saddened, and in utter disbelief. My mind immediately turned to thinking of ways that I could help. In those early days, there was not much more to do than to visit the hospital, and watch my very brave friend work at coming to terms with her diagnosis, the resultant surgery, and the ongoing treatment.

I watched as she underwent chemotherapy and radiotherapy. I went with her to my hairdresser to find a wig that might suit her as she dealt with the confronting experience of losing her hair. We laughed and cried as she tried on a variety of wigs that were so very different from her straight, shiny mid-brown hair. We laughed and cried again when she realised that she could not stand the feel of the expensive wig she had purchased. It was too hot, too itchy, and just not okay! I watched her embrace, as bravely and gracefully as she could, her hair loss, the chemotherapy, the radiotherapy, the nausea, and the loss of control she had over so many elements of her life.

My beautiful, heroic, and very determined friend fought just so hard to stay alive. She battled for seven long years against the dreadful disease that eventually took her life. In that time, she achieved a great deal. She partnered with her husband to raise their young family of four. She formed an interior design business with another friend. She travelled and holidayed with her family. She still managed to entertain beautifully when she was well enough. She read, she gardened, and she tried to stay as fit and healthy as she could. Did she often discuss her diagnosis, treatment, and uncertain future with me? The answer is no. We had an unspoken understanding that our conversations, connection, and catch ups, were the things that mattered most in our relationship. It was important that we talked about the everyday things that bonded us together as friends.

In my eyes, she was a living, breathing example of Kintsugi. In her own unique, and very stylish way, she took her illness – the cracks, chips, dents, and broken parts of her life – and mended them with threads of gold. She took her extremely difficult challenges and setbacks, and turned them into something that made her extraordinarily beautiful. She didn't need to speak of the repairs she had made to herself, her bravery and brilliance were there on show, evident for all to see.

At the end of her life, she was so fragile but, at the same time, so incredibly strong. I was privileged to be with her and with her family on the day she died. To this day, she remains a constant inspiration in my life. Was she aware that she was applying the ancient art of Kintsugi to her being? Almost certainly not. Did I know of the art form back in the 1990s? Absolutely not. But now, with the distance of many years, and with the knowledge and wisdom that comes with age and experience, I can see it was the golden joinery that she so bravely applied to her life, and to her self-leadership map, that made her a rare and special treasure that shone so brightly.

Life has cracked me open on more than one occasion. At these times, I have been stressed, anxious, disappointed, frightened, rejected, or on my knees, breaking and falling apart. One of the times when I remember wondering whether I'd ever get back up off the floor, was at the end of 2017 when the period of burnout shook me to my core.

I didn't recognise myself. I didn't like who I saw when I looked in the mirror. I didn't understand who I was anymore, and I couldn't see how I'd ever be the same again. The truth is, I wasn't ever exactly the same again. I was changed by my experiences. I was changed by my fear and anxiety. However, I knew that with support, I had to begin to make sense of what had happened to me. And then, tentatively and with openness and vulnerability, I had to begin to put myself back together.

That is exactly what I did. I sought the help of professionals who guided me to understand that the expectations I had of myself were unsustainable over a lifetime. I had expected myself to be strong, to cope, and to always carry on regardless. I was broken. I'd experienced burnout. I had fallen apart.

The process of healing began with my local doctor, who pretty quickly ascertained that I needed some medication to calm my overstretched nervous system so that I could begin to breathe and function again. This chemical assistance helped me to calm and to feel a little better. The regular visits to my kind, supportive, and encouraging psychologist helped me to share so many of the challenging and heartbreaking experiences that I had held onto for so long. She listened compassionately, with interest and respect. She taught me simple strategies to help ground myself when I felt the panic and anxiety begin to rise in me. These two steps, attending my doctor and engaging a psychologist, gave me the space and support I needed to draw on the resources that I already had within me, to begin the process of healing.

From early November until the end of January, when the new school year commenced, I actively engaged in extreme self-care. I tried many things as I attempted to regain my strength, my confidence, and my sense of equilibrium. Here is a list of self-care actions that supported my recovery. They helped light the pathway on my deeply personal journey back to strength and wellbeing.

My Self Care List

- I prayed simple heartfelt prayers each time I felt shaky and frightened.
- I wrote a gratitude journal, where I simply expressed my thanks for three good things (no matter how tiny) that I had experienced that day.
- I bathed myself in sunshine each day.
- I walked in nature, consciously taking in the beauty that was all around me.
- I spent time on the beach and in the water.
- I actively practised mindfulness when completing the simplest of tasks.
- I pushed myself each day to have some small social connection with people other than my family – this may have been a simple smile or hello as I walked, or it may have been a coffee at the local café with some new people I'd recently met.
- I ate healthy, life-giving food.
- I kept my body hydrated.
- I abstained from alcohol.
- I treated myself to an afternoon sleep whenever I felt tired.
- I expressed my creativity through writing, and through making spaces in my home as lovely as I could.

This three-month period of healing reinforced, for me, the things that my intellectual mind already knew. Here I was, a person who had studied Positive Psychology, who knew the research about creating wellbeing, was now realising firsthand that these actions actually work when you are broken and feeling very shaky and low! I learned that these simple tools are some of the building blocks to recovery, increased self-confidence, and are important tools in healthy, life-giving self-leadership.

Before I knew it, it was time to return to the school where I worked as principal. It was not without uncertainty and fear that I prepared to address the staff on the first day of the 2018 school year. As I rose to speak to the expectant group, I thought I knew exactly what I was going to say. I was going to thank them for their work in my absence. I was going to tell them that I felt so much better now, and then I was going to tell them that I had returned to start the new year fresh and ready to go.

As I spoke, my story of stress, brokenness and fear tumbled from my lips in an honest and heartfelt way. I told them of the slow recovery I was making. I told them that I was using every tool that I had in my toolkit to help me along the way. I told them that, for so many reasons, I had come to a time and place in my life where my mind and body told me that I needed to stop, to rest, to seek support, and to rebuild again. As I finished my address and we moved on to the business of the day, I felt just a little vulnerable, but I also felt proud. I felt stronger. I felt glad.

Throughout that day, I was approached on three occasions by different staff members who came to tell me that they marvelled at what I had done earlier in the day. They couldn't believe that I'd been so honest, made myself so vulnerable, and shared my very personal story with them. I explained that it had actually felt so powerful for me to share my experience. I wanted them all to know that we need to take care of ourselves, and that even though we often require the support of others, we are ultimately responsible for our own wellbeing and progress.

What I had begun to do, and what I continue to do each day, is to polish, nurture and be proud of the threads of gold that hold my story, my heartaches, and my life lessons, because they are the golden bonds that hold me together. These golden bonds help make me the work of art I have become. The seams of golden repairs, that put me back together, are to be proud of and celebrated. They are to be polished and treasured. They help weave together the tapestry of my life. My golden, more successful moments may shine on their own, but the weaker, more vulnerable, broken moments, are the ones that make me the unique and interesting person that I now celebrate!

> *"I dare you to take off the mask of perfection and show up as you are. Feel the freedom, the relief, the lightness. Because when we are real, that's when we actually heal. And those around us just might heal, too."*
>
> Ashley Hetherington

As with any craft, it takes time, practice and patience to develop. I strongly commend to you the idea that in life's challenging moments, when you are broken down, the practice of the actions contained in my self-care list will support you as you navigate the challenges you face. Even more than this, if you incorporate as many of these practices as you can into your daily routine, you will find a sense of calm, a sense of buoyancy, and a sense of joy as these simple practices become part of your daily way of living.

We cannot control everything that happens to us, nor can we always control how we react. What I am confident of is that all we can do is to control the controllables so that, as much as possible, we make space, we make choices, and we choose the way forward despite whatever hurdle is in front of us.

I am currently living through a time of great challenge and great change as my sisters, brother, and I, try very hard to support our mum who is experiencing rapidly increasing dementia. This cruel disease is robbing her of her short-term memory, so that days, dates, objects, and important possessions are 'lost' somewhere, and we struggle to help resolve and ease these very confronting challenges.

Often I see the fear, doubt and confusion etched on her face, as she presents herself as 'dressed and ready to go' to a family event that may be four days away. We have no idea where this journey will lead us as we continue to love and provide increasing support to our mother. There are many times that I am grateful that I do not know what the journey ahead will look like.

What I do know, with every fibre of my being, is that I need to look after myself in order to be able to play my part in looking after her. Self-care is a vital strategy for living a full, satisfying, and authentic life. I am aware that nutrition, hydration, exercise, mindfulness, journalling, prayer, and gratitude are the practices, and positive, life-giving habits that allow me to manage this extremely challenging and heartbreaking part of being a daughter who loves her mother, and who is watching her slowly disappear.

Some might say that I am deludedly playing the role of Pollyanna by stating so emphatically that these strategies help make the terrifying and heartbreaking a little easier to manage and to bear. I, however, know that I must go on this journey with my mum, and I must navigate it in the healthiest, most positive way that I can so that I emerge, on the other side, forever changed but intact and able to go on. I believe that this is my version of Kintsugi at work in my life.

Self-Leadership Map Signpost No:5
Self-awareness + self-acceptance + learning + growth = Recognising and nurturing your more vulnerable self.

Great Coaching Questions About Brokenness, Resilience
What factors do you feel contribute to your ability to remain flexible when faced with a setback?
How can you apply that to your current challenge?

A Piece of Wisdom from Positive Psychology
How do we find healing in our brokenness? What is brokenness asking of us? We remember our closest ally – the calming presence of our breath. We bring awareness to our varying moods, seeking equanimity. We do our inner work, perhaps turn to a trusted friend or therapist. We seek community. We take refuge in the wise perspective of impermanence. Psychology Today magazine

Chapter Seven
How Big Is Your Why?

Find Your Meaning and Purpose

"A noble purpose inspires sacrifice, stimulates innovation and encourages perseverance."

Gary Hamel

It seems to me that life is a journey. Now I know that is not an original thought. I also realise that I'm not the only person who has used the word 'journey' as a metaphor for life. Life is a series of moments – some big, some small, some related, connected and linear, and others, just moments that sometimes add colour and texture to the fabric of our lives. Ever since human beings have been able to record their thoughts and their wonderings, people have written about their search for meaning.

Many want to know why they are here, and what their purpose is. In fact, most human beings have times in their lives where they wonder about their purpose, their impact on the lives of their loved ones, on their communities and, sometimes, even on the wider world. Others drift through life enjoying some moments, despising others, and being caught up in the mundane blandness of the moments in between. There are others who simply live day to day, just allowing life to happen to them and all around them.

I've never wanted to be that person. I've always wanted direction, clarity, and purpose. As a teenager, I was always interested in, and thrived on, deep conversations and on recording my thoughts and feelings in prose and poetry. People often commented that they loved the 'deep' conversations they had with me. They would sometimes comment that they loved the way I just 'got' them. They said they loved my perspective on life.

I have fond memories of being a 16-year-old girl perched on a clifftop at Airey's Inlet in Victoria, writing in what I would now describe as a journal. Thoughts, dreams and heartaches were all poured out, and recorded in my own heartfelt style. At the time I enjoyed sharing many of these writings with one of my closest friends. I enjoyed the fact that she shared her writing with me. The conversations that stemmed from this sharing were both intimate and beautiful.

Even as a young woman, words, both written and spoken, have been powerful in my life. Over the years, nothing has changed. I believe more strongly than ever that communication, connection, presenting, and coaching are my super powers. They are my tools, my skills and my vehicle for keeping me on the road as I head towards my 'true north'.

It is interesting to me that, all these years on, I am still working to further develop these skills so that I can progress my career into the future. These same skills will also support my life journey for as long as I walk the planet. I have used my communication skills as a daughter, partner, parent, friend, teacher, principal, and coach. As I look forward to creating new ways to add value, meaning, greater purpose, and fulfilment to my life, I find it stimulating and worthwhile to continue trying to refine my life's purpose. I want self-confidence and self-leadership to shine from me. I want others, who seek to clarify and grow their own life's purpose, to see that I really 'walk my talk' and that what I say can be of practical use in their lives. I want to help other people on their journeys towards living successful lives that are full of energy, purpose and joy.

> *"If it is your calling, it will keep calling you."*
>
> Anonymous

At this stage of my life, my life purpose is defined by the following statement:

> *"To inspire people of all ages to realise their self-worth, potential, and power. I encourage and support them to develop committed self-leadership. I want them to know that it is not too early, nor is it too late, to step into their own powerful purpose and truly live."*

In attempting to define and write a mission statement that will empower you, and drive you forward towards your 'true north', I think it is helpful to first become really playful and to let your imagination, and your heartfelt hopes and dreams run wild. At this stage, you should say to yourself, "I am going to create the movie of my life, just as I want it to be. I am going to create a movie where I am the hero".

I encourage you to become the director and the producer of this movie. I urge you to be brave enough to create a compelling vision of your life as you imagine just how you want it to be. Make your vision big, make it bright, add detail, and colour, and music to it, just as if this vision is a movie playing in your head. Once you have done this important work, you should be able to come close to putting into words the mission of the hero in your movie.

Write Your Own Mission Statement

Have you ever considered writing your own mission statement? I imagine that many of you have not. The words 'mission statement' sound so important, and do you know what? I truly believe they are. Take some time to think about the people, including celebrities and others, who have been famous throughout history. Think also about some of the companies and brands that you know well. Do you know what they stand for? Do you know anything about their mission in life?

Let's look at some well-known examples:

- **Oprah Winfrey** – "To be a teacher. And to be known for inspiring my students to be more than they thought they could be."

- **Matthew McConaughey** – "To empower high school students by providing them with the tools to lead active lives and make healthy choices for a better future."
- **Ash Barty** – "Helping to provide opportunities for First Nations youth in sport and education."
- **Neil Daniher** – "There's always opportunity, and my opportunity is to fight MND. And that's allowed me to prevail. It's allowed me to find purpose, to transcend what's happening to me."
- **Nike** – "To bring inspiration and innovation to every athlete in the world."
- **Tesla** – "To accelerate the world's transition to sustainable energy."
- **Google** – "To organise the world's information and make it universally accessible and useful."

Each of these mission statements is highly aspirational, yet very clear and grounded in purpose. They make the person's or organisation's mission crystal clear. I believe the two keys to a great and highly effective mission statement are:

1. It must have a 'super clear' message that speaks directly to your heart.
2. It must inspire you to take action towards fulfilling that mission every day of your life.

In light of these statements, there are many things to consider when writing your own mission statement. It is important to consider the following points:

- What lights you up?
- What brings up deep emotion when you speak about it?
- What are you passionate about?

- What gives you energy, clarity, and drive?
- What are your values and beliefs?
- What are your talents and skills?
- Who do you want to be?
- How do you want to be remembered?
- What contribution do you want to make to the world?
- What will be your legacy after you've gone?
- If you were listening to a family member or friend delivering your eulogy, what would they say about you?
- What would you like to hear?

Record your ideas and thoughts in the table

What Are Your Passions?	What Are Your Values?	What Are Your Skills and Talents?	What Contribution is Your Contribution?	How Will You Be Remembered?

It is important to remember that your mission statement is just that, yours! It is the deeply personal message that you send to yourself every day. Your mission may be something deeply personal that you hold close to your heart, or it may be something you may want to share with the world. Either way, it should be something that excites, motivates, and moves you. It will be a message that you connect deeply with, and want to take action towards every single day of your life. This mission will be your guiding light, your 'true north', and your reason for being. It is your life's mission.

My advice to you is to play with words, ideas, and feelings, until you have a statement that feels deeply personal and is yours alone. Your personal mission statement will eventually be something you can call to mind and state out loud.

Imagine stepping into an elevator and you have only the time it takes to move from the ground floor to the top floor to deliver your 'pitch', your 'buy line', your mission statement to an audience. Will your statement be believable, authentic, and heart felt enough to create interest, curiosity, and an emotional response in those listening? If you were actually selling your mission statement to others, would you be able to persuade them to buy? Whether you want to be the C.E.O of a company, an artist, an entrepreneur, or simply the best person, parent, partner or friend you can be, how do you write a statement that will enliven your heart, inspire your mind, and call you to take positive action, and practise authentic self-leadership every day of your life?

I cannot stress enough that this process is well worth undertaking. So undertake it with all the love, thought, care, and time you can muster. You may not like your first few attempts but, if you persist, you will create a statement that inspires you. You are the C.E.O of your life. You are your own most important project. Design a vision and a statement that you love. Let it be one that motivates and moves you every day of your life.

Once you can name your mission with ease, and see it in your mind's eye as though it is an action movie, it is most important that you begin to live as though the vision you have created is real. Imagine that the mission you have set for yourself is your top priority. Begin every day by imagining, practising, and acting as though you have already become the person you aspire to be.

As much as possible, think, learn, speak, move, eat, save, invest, and respond like the person who is the hero in the movie of your life. Act as your ideal self. Act as though you have already arrived at your final destination. Act as though you are living and breathing into this new person who is your ideal self. Strive to be the hero of your own real life action movie.

The more you can think and act in this way, the more natural it will feel. It will be like trying on new clothes or a new pair of shoes. You will be able to see how they fit, and whether you truly like the style of the life you are consciously creating. You will see how it feels to be the star! You will see how it feels to truly live your life's mission.

One of the most wonderful ways I have heard this idea expressed comes from the well-known American actor and politician, Arnold Schwarzeneggar. He said:

> *"Create a vision of who you want to be, and then live into that picture as if it is already true."*
> Arnold Schwarzeneggar

In more recent years, especially since I realised that I had a book inside me that was waiting to be written, I have taken this approach in my life. When I began to act this way, I felt a little shy, a little uncomfortable, and a little awkward to say that I was a writer. My inner critic used to appear like clockwork, to sit on my shoulder and whisper unsettlingly, disruptive things to me. I'd hear her voice say, "What are you doing?" What are you telling yourself?" "Don't you dare think that you are good enough to tell other people that you are writing a book." "You are a teacher and a school principal and you'll never be anything more than that!" "What makes you think that you can change and do this work at your age?"

In the face of this negative self-talk, one of the first things I did was to adjust my original list of belief statements to include the things I wanted to be. You can see in the table below that I added the statement, "*I adapt to change and learn new things*". I then elaborated by adding four statements that expressed more fully the work I want to do. These statements are: *"I am a communicator." "I am a connector." "I am a writer." "I am a coach."*

My Original List	My Additions	My New List
I am strong	I adapt to change and learn new things	I am strong
I am beautiful	I am capable	I am beautiful
I am resilient	I am confident	I am confident
I treat myself with respect, care and kindness	I am resilient	I am resilient
I treat others with kindness and respect	I am a writer	I adapt to change and learn new things
I am ENOUGH	I am a coach	I treat myself with respect, care and kindness
		I treat others with kindness and respect
		I am a communicator

		I am a connector
		I am a writer
		I am a coach
		I am ENOUGH

I had been working on this book in quite a sporadic fashion over the past two years. I realised that, in the busyness of my life with my family, and my career demanding and deserving a great deal of my time, my writing always took second place. I knew that I was 'dragging the chain' and that my book may well have never been more than a half-written manuscript. I innately knew that I had to take myself in hand and get on with the job. I gave myself a mental 'kick' and got to work.

I know that I am a work in progress. I am writing this section of my book early on a warm, wet Saturday morning. I have made a commitment to live as if I am already a published author. I have set a goal, and made myself a very strong promise that I will complete my first draft of this book by the end of 2024. I connect online fortnightly with my mentor who checks in with me, keeps me honest, and encourages me to keep working towards my end date. My mentor's name is Andrew Jobling. He works with, and encourages, aspiring writers who want to publish their writing. He works with people who want to become published authors. When I work with him, I feel even more focused and energised. Speaking with Andrew fuels me to step even further into my own personal power, and move closer to the completion of my first draft. Through my work with him, I move closer to being able to present my work to a publisher.

My mentor recently suggested to me that I take on a challenge called the Permanent Positive Change Challenge. Together we explored the notion of habit creation. I was already aware of the widely held belief that it takes 21 days to form a new habit. He challenged that idea saying there was another belief that habit creation takes much longer, in fact it can take anywhere between 63 and 254 days.

The coach in me already knew a great deal about creating tiny habits that build towards greater, more positive, and more lasting change. What amazed me was the simple practice my mentor suggested I follow. It was just so powerful. He presented a simple chart that required me to think about the habit or change I wanted to make. He said that human beings first have a **thought** about what it is they want to change, then they experience **emotion** about the change they want to make. If they decide to **act** to make the change happen, they must start to build a routine and then, after **consistent practice**, they will experience change, progress, growth and **SUCCESS**!

My mentor suggested that I write down the permanent positive change I wished to make. He made it very clear that I should write down the **action** I wanted to take that would lead towards my desired outcome or goal. So I began the process of describing what I wanted to achieve. I knew it was about committing to writing each and every day. I knew that I often made easy, believable, and comfortable excuses about why it was taking me so long to complete my book. I knew that this was the situation I wanted to change, so I asked myself this question, *"How can I love and care for my family, fully execute my role as a primary school principal, and still complete a first draft of my book by the end of 2024?"*

I thought for a while and then the answer came to me. The answer was simple. My supportive, and often very useful, inner voice asked me this question, *"If this is so important to you, why don't you dedicate a set amount of time each day for uninterrupted writing?"* If I was truly honest with myself, the only answer I could come up with was that maybe I wasn't quite as dedicated as I often professed to be! Maybe I was waiting for a great burst of energy and inspiration, or perhaps even a miracle, that would come my way, and my book would magically be complete! I have lived long enough to know that this idea was simply wishful or deluded thinking. This spasmodic way of approaching my project was not useful, not resourceful and, to be perfectly honest, going nowhere fast!

I made a simple decision to shape a plan for permanent, positive change. I wrote the change I wanted to achieve as an action statement. I wrote it on the chart that my mentor had given me. I stuck the chart on the wall of our study near the computer where I worked each day. Although I didn't record the time of day that I would write, I planned to work early in the morning when I knew I was at my best. I have always been an early riser so this was not a particular challenge for me. I have risen at 5.00 am for many, many years. I have done this for several reasons:

- My home is quiet so I have time and space for myself.
- I can complete my routine of checking emails, writing school newsletters, editing student reports, and carrying out my morning rituals.
- It gives me the time and space later in the morning to attend to the day to day matters that go with leading others, and effectively running a school.
- It also allows me time to go for my morning walk that always enhances how I feel and act for the remainder of my day.

This is what I wrote as my action for permanent positive change: *I write my book for sixty minutes each day.* – Notice that my action is written in the **present tense.**

Instead of rising at 5.00 am, I set my alarm for 4.00 am so that I could achieve my plan. I can hear many of you shriek in horror at the thought of getting out of a comfortable bed at 4.00 am each day. I told myself that if I wanted my first draft of the book completed by the end of 2024, I would have to make some sacrifices in the present. My days were always full when I rose at 5.00 am, so I knew that I needed to find an extra sixty minutes for myself. I asked myself, *"Where will I find the time?"* The answer was easy for me. I knew I would find it at the start of the day.

As I write this section of the book, I have been working on my habit change plan for 39 days in a row. Each morning when my alarm sounds, I use a strategy that has worked so well for me in other situations. I employed 'The Five Second Rule' made famous by American motivational writer, speaker and coach, Mel Robbins.

Have you ever seen a rocket being launched? Have you ever heard the countdown before the launch? You know the one, 5… 4… 3… 2…1… Lift off! We have 'Lift Off'! Do you think that those in Mission Control, who launch the rocket, know exactly what their mission is before they begin? I am certain that they do. When employing 'The Five Second Rule', I behave in exactly the same way as the people at Mission Control:

- I tell myself what I am about to do – *I am going to launch myself out of bed immediately after the count of one.*
- I walk to my study, look at the time, take three deep cleansing breaths, set a timer on my phone and then I write for 60 minutes.
- I colour the next empty square on my Permanent Positive Change chart, and go on with the rest of my day – *my first important achievement of the day completed just after 5.00 am!*

What has amazed me during this process of change is the power of the chart. I could never have imagined that a piece of paper, stuck to my wall, would be such an important motivational tool, and a strong visual reminder of what I have achieved as I worked towards my goal. I have found myself feeling compelled and excited to get up in the early morning to work on my book, and to colour in one tiny square as I moved towards

63 unbroken days of writing. While it was one thing to write a section of my book each day, and to colour in a small square on my chart, it was quite another when I realised that the act of writing each day was moving me in the direction of my dreams.

The act of writing each day gave me confidence, and the wonderful feeling of both momentum and authenticity, as I moved closer towards my dream of completing my first book. A wonderful speaker, coach and author, Colleen Callander, with whom I had the privilege of working, once told me that a published book is a very impressive and useful business card. When you can hold your published work in your hand, and present it to someone else, you can proudly say, "This is what I know. This is my experience. I can speak and present and teach from this body of work."

When I reflect upon the personal growth I have made during this time, I feel immensely proud of myself and of my efforts. I am illustrating to myself on a daily basis that I can evolve, change, and grow. I don't have to leave everything I currently am behind. I am simply adding to my repertoire of knowledge and skills I have to offer the world. What I am realising and learning, on a daily basis, is that it is never too late to try something new. It is never too late to pursue your passions and your dreams.

Can you think of a time in your life where you've wanted to make a change or, perhaps, achieve something completely new? I feel fairly certain that you can. Perhaps you wanted to:

- Build a regular fitness routine.
- Save for a particular purpose.
- Lose a few kilos and adopt a healthier approach to diet and exercise.
- Work on your relationship.
- Change your mind-set about going to work each day.

- Change your career.
- Start a passion project.
- Build a side hustle.

> *"Who you are becoming is more important than who you've been."*
>
> Joe Clementi

If you decide to try to change a behaviour or habit you currently have, or if you decide to introduce a new practice or behaviour into your life, I strongly suggest that you ask yourself the following questions, and then use the change chart that I have developed and shared below.

Questions:

- What is one positive change I would like to make in my life?
- How will it move me closer towards being my ideal self?
- How will it help me achieve what I want?
- What attitudes and behaviours did I consistently demonstrate the last time I made a successful and positive change?

Use the chart below as a strong visual reminder of your change journey, your progress and your ultimate success.

What change would I like to create?

Why is this change important to me?

The Self-Leadership Change Chart

Action																					
First 21 Days																					
Day	1	2	3	4	5	6	7	8	9	10	11	12	13	14	15	16	17	18	19	20	21
Second 21 Days																					
Day	1	2	3	4	5	6	7	8	9	10	11	12	13	14	15	16	17	18	19	20	21
Third 21 Days																					
Day	1	2	3	4	5	6	7	8	9	10	11	12	13	14	15	16	17	18	19	20	21

HOW BIG IS YOUR WHY?

Each of the questions I have asked require you to start with the end in mind. It is important to see yourself, in your mind's eye, doing the exact thing you have set as the element/project/way of being that you want to create or to change. Play the movie in your head. Make it as colourful, bright, and compelling as you can. Play the movie with the volume turned up loud so that, as well as being able to see yourself, you can actually hear yourself actively creating and living the change you imagine.

When you think, plan, work, and live in this way, as though you are the central character and the star of your own movie, you improve the quality of your life and your relationships, each and every day. You have found your purpose and your reason for being. You are taking positive action to elevate every aspect and moment of your life each and every day. Your purpose is clear. You know the way. And, as you look back in the rear-view mirror of your life, you will see behind you achievement and effort, success and failure, growth, progress, and a life that has been truly lived. Go for it! Write the script. Call action on the set. Launch your rocket from mission control. Don't wait to be perfect. Be the star of your own brilliant life.

Self-Leadership Map Signpost No:6
Purpose + passion + practise = Self-mastery + meaning + success.

Great Coaching Questions About Purpose, Mission and Self-Love
What is the vision you hold for yourself?
Who are you when you give yourself full permission?
What messages from your inner critic are you listening to and allowing to hold you back?
If you were to let go of X belief, what might be possible?
How will you amplify your core value of X today?
What new perspectives could you explore/stand in/engage in?

A Piece of Wisdom from Positive Psychology
An intrinsic human quality is the search for **meaning**, and the need to have a sense of value and worth. Seligman (2012) discussed meaning as belonging and/or serving something greater than ourselves. Having a purpose in life helps individuals focus on what is really important in the face of significant challenge or adversity.

Chapter Eight
Fear Or Love

The Choice is Yours

"In any given moment, we have two options: to step forward into growth or step back into safety."

Abraham Maslow

Have you ever dreamt of doing things just a little bit differently, or perhaps even trying something completely new? This could be as simple as a new hairstyle, or as challenging as changing your career, leaving a friendship or a relationship that you recognise is no longer good for you. Decision making is often tricky and, sometimes, it's downright hard. We all make thousands of decisions every day – what to eat, what to wear, who to talk to, what to buy, whether to exercise, and the list goes on.

Many of these decisions are almost unconscious choices that allow our lives to run along a mostly familiar and comfortable track. Sometimes we are called to make bigger, more important decisions, and we can feel cautious, stuck, overwhelmed, and unsure of exactly which move to make next.

Brave self-leadership calls for us to wake up. It calls us to step into the amazing power of self-love. This form of love is both wonderful and powerful when we choose to embrace it. Does it come easily and naturally? No, not always. Does it grow and develop the more we focus on the brilliant and unique human beings we actually are? Yes, absolutely!

> *"Fear doesn't control us by dominating our emotions. It controls us by quietly convincing us that our comfort is more important than our happiness."*
>
> Mark Manson

I can hear your next question, "If that is the truth, then how do I lead myself to the place where I can grow in self-love?" "How do I let go of the nagging fears, doubts and stories I tell myself that constantly hold me back?" Let me tell you about part of my journey to greater self-love, self-respect, inner peace, and freedom. As I mentioned earlier in my story, belief statements are among the powerful tools that helped me reprogram some of my negative internal chatter and unresourceful thinking.

There have been many times in my life when I have had to quieten the voice of my inner critic. When I say inner critic, I'm sure you know exactly what I mean. My inner critic often appears to sit on my shoulder, and persists in whispering into my ear all the reasons why I should remain exactly as I am.

She tells me that changing, growing, and making a different decision, will be too hard. She tells me I don't have the knowledge and the skills to step up, and make a choice that will actually benefit me. She tells me that I don't have the money, or the resources, to make the changes, or take the opportunities that are in front of me. She tells me that it's not the right time. She has told me that I'm too young. She tells me I am too old. She so cleverly points out all the people in the world who are better, more skilled, more talented, more beautiful, and more worthy than me.

She is so persuasive when she constantly reminds me of all the reasons why things won't work, and why the opportunities in front of me are not actually meant for me. She tells me I'm not ready. She reminds me that I need to stay safe. She says that I need to just stay in my lane and remain exactly as I am, or everything might just fall apart. She is the voice of fear. She is the voice who always wants to maintain the status quo. She wants me to stay stuck.

A wonderful example of my inner critic at play is when I was making the decision to go to university and study to become a teacher. I was 33 years old. Our children were aged 14, 9, 6, 5 and 3. My husband worked six days per week. I was caught up in the busyness of school lunches and school fundraising, of weekend sport with our two older sons, and then, of course, the usual round of birthday parties, play dates, and family and social commitments that kept me extremely busy. I was also influenced by a strong narrative that ran in my family. This narrative told the story that mothers should always be with their children. They did not work full-time. They did not study.

This message was strong and, at the time, I guess it was completely understandable. My own beautiful mum had lost her mother when she was just ten years old. She was the eldest of seven children who were separated from each other, and sent to live with relatives in different parts of Victoria. Their lives were not easy, and there was no mother to go to for comfort, advice, and support.

Because of this story, and the beliefs that were attached to it, I was led to believe that having someone care for my children, while I went off to study, was not a wise, fair or kind decision. Although it was never said out loud, the message seemed to be that going to study would be a selfish choice. The messaging was very clear, I should put my children's needs first and, therefore, mine at the very end of the list.

My inner critic always showed up to reinforce the message. She was the voice of fear. She wanted me to stay stuck. Her voice whispered in my ear at all times of the day and night. She said, "Don't be so selfish, you know that children always come first!" She also regularly reminded me that my mother would never understand, or approve of, what I wanted to do. Despite these daily reminders that I should just 'stay in my lane' and be a responsible, unselfish mother, another voice whispered in my other ear. This was the voice of my ideal, or higher self. This was the voice of the woman I wanted to become. This was the voice of love. Her voice gently, yet persistently, asked me, "What if you do go on to study?" "What if you let yourself grow and blossom and change?" "What will this brave decision do for your hard-working husband, your beautiful children and most importantly, what will it do for you?"

After sitting with this difficult decision for far too long, I finally allowed the voice of my ideal self to speak more loudly than the voice of fear. At times, when I felt brave enough, I began to have conversations with people who worked in education, people who were doing the work I wanted to do. Did I call a university and make an inquiry? No. Instead, the cautious me made small, tentative steps in the direction of my dreams by talking to some of the teachers at my children's primary school.

One day, the principal of my children's school, a generous and wise Catholic nun, asked me whether I had ever considered working in a primary school classroom as a volunteer. She suggested that I should come to school once a week, and work with a variety of teachers. She recommended that I keep a journal of the work I did, the things I observed, and what I learned from each experience.

After a month or two of showing up, engaging in learning, and thoroughly enjoying the experience, the principal asked me whether I thought I'd like to enrol in a mid-year intake at university. Oh my goodness! My heart raced; my head spun. My inner critic began placing every doubt and obstacle imaginable in my path. I told myself that I couldn't possibly do that. My ideal self was calmer, warmer and more supportive. She often whispered to me, "Yes, but what if you did?"

> *"Anxiety happens when you think you have to figure out everything all at once. Breathe. You're strong. You got this. Take it day by day."*
>
> Karen Salmonsohn

When I eventually calmed myself, I spoke with my husband and, after some careful consideration and some strong encouragement from him, I decided to go for it. I was going to try. I completed the enrolment form and attended an interview, where I spoke passionately about my reasons for wanting to become a teacher. I was absolutely delighted when I was accepted to study two subjects in my first semester. With the support of my beautiful sister and later, a wonderful friend, I began as an undergraduate at university.

Could I actually believe that the girl, who had left school at the tender age of 17, to have her precious son was now on her way to completing the education she had left unfinished in 1975? No, not really! I was a grown woman attending university as a 'mature age student'. It had been 16 years since I had been inside a classroom.

The thought of showing up as an older student was somewhat daunting to say the least. But 'show up' I did, and I soon saw that I could engage in the lectures and tutorials. I seemed to be accepted by other students, and I was not the only person among the first-year students who was older than 18. The juggle was real, but the pride, enjoyment and new learning were worth every struggle. At 33 years of age, I was finally on the path to an exciting and rewarding career.

You may wonder what my mother made of my decision. Once I took the step, she was always supportive in helping out wherever our children were concerned. As time went on, it seemed as though she could better understand the choices that I made. I know that, at the time of writing this book, after a 26-year teaching career, she is just so proud of who I am, and of what I do. The most important element of decision-making is not what others think of you, but what you think about yourself and what you choose to claim as yours. When decisions are worked through, and are made in alignment with your values and beliefs, you are on the path of true self-leadership, fulfilment and success.

There are so many times in our lives when we allow ourselves to choose fear over love. Choosing fear involves staying stuck, and often comes from our need to 'play small' and to choose safety over discovery and opportunity. I can think of so many times in my life where I have allowed fear to be my dominant and ruling emotion. I have allowed fear to hold me back. Through choosing fear, I have missed opportunities for fun, joy, growth, new learning, and new friendships.

I have chosen fear when:

- I let myself miss an opportunity to try a new physical activity through the fear of looking silly, and not being able to do it at my first attempt.
- I stick to a diet of comfort, rather than one that is so much better suited to my body, and my ultimate health and wellbeing.
- I continued old patterns in relation to my finances, because I've told myself stories about both the fear of 'not having enough' and the thought of 'losing it all'.
- I missed opportunities to explore new learning and new connections through the fear of admitting that I don't possess a certain knowledge base or skill set.

As I look back to times where I allowed fear to rule both my head and my heart, I feel sorry that I missed so many opportunities to learn, to grow, and to eventually shine. My best advice to you, if you are a person who often chooses to 'stay stuck' through fear, is to think again. Create a belief statement or two that you can add to your daily mantra that you repeat in front of the mirror each morning.

These are the statements I included in my daily mantra of beliefs about having the courage and the determination to choose love over fear:

- I am strong
- I am confident
- I am capable
- I am resilient
- I adapt to change and learn new things

In my role as a school principal, there are situations that arise from time to time that cause me to engage in conversations and meetings that are really challenging. When managing staff, finding the courage to hold a discussion with a staff member about underperformance, or not following expected protocols and practices, is always an extremely challenging one. Attending meetings with angry, disgruntled, or disappointed parents is also challenging. Sometimes, in situations such as these, it is easy to fall into the trap of allowing fear to rule my words and actions. It is easy to weaken, and to avoid the necessary conversation with a staff member. It is easy to allow the parent to look at things only from their perspective, and not to look at the entire situation.

What I have come to realise is that 'easy' is not often 'best'. I know that when I let fear rule my head, my heart, and therefore my decisions, I always feel disappointed, unsettled and, later, often frustrated with myself. Another byproduct of letting fear be my ruler is that the situations I avoided addressing appropriately often continue. The staff member continues to act in ways that don't match expectations, or follow the set protocols for being a member of our school team. The parent goes away thinking that their perspective of a situation is the only one. They think that the problem is resolved. They think that they have had their way, and their say. They possibly see me as a 'pushover'.

What I know for sure is that letting fear rule your decisions, and your heart, robs you of so many opportunities to step into your own personal power, and to choose courage. Fear is often associated with memory, perhaps a memory of a previous experience that was traumatic, an experience that didn't go as you had planned in your mind's eye, or that you didn't enjoy in any way, shape or form. Past experiences will always influence our thinking when faced with decision making in new, unfamiliar and often challenging situations.

We can choose to let fear be the anchor that roots us to a static position, or we can choose love as the motor, the fuel, the energy, and the drive, to propel us forward into new ways of thinking and living that are profoundly more life-giving and resourceful. So, I hear you ask, "How do I do just that?"

There are many ways to change your thinking and move away from fear. Once you start thinking and acting from a place of curiosity and self-love, you will find your life will become easier to manage, and far more rewarding. You can begin by:

- Accepting that you are human, vulnerable and fallible. You can accept that you will continue to make mistakes and get things wrong. Regardless, you can always show yourself compassion and kindness.
- Understand that even though you choose to treat yourself with kindness and compassion, and not with fear and regret, you will still encounter times of struggle. With self-love as your driving force, you will recognise, and celebrate, the progress you are making with each small positive step you take.
- View other people with the same understanding and compassion that you now apply to yourself. You will never really know what

- other people are going through in any situation. You cannot change them, you can only develop and change yourself.
- Let go of past mistakes. Set your compass in a new direction away from the choices and decisions, people and events that were difficult or that held you back.
- Make taking care of your body a priority for each day that you live. Your body is the sacred vehicle in which the 'essential you' lives your life.
- Decide you are worth the investment and the effort. Do not let the opinions of others define you, or hold you back. You were born to thrive.
- Practise gratitude every day. Live with an attitude of gratitude. A grateful, open heart will lead you to people, places, and opportunities that will provide you with even more of what you want in life.
- Become self-aware enough to notice when certain thoughts, beliefs, practices and habits are no longer useful, or not supporting your growth and development. Let them go.
- Use your values and beliefs to set healthy, protective boundaries so that you are free to move in the direction of your dreams.
- Choose to be present. Being fully present means showing up as the best version of yourself, wherever you are and whatever you do. Showing up as the best version of yourself means that, even when you are alone and nobody is watching, you live your values. This is integrity at work.
- Speak up when you need to, or when you want to. Your voice is important. Ask for what you need. Use kind, clear and honest language. You have a right to be heard.

- Look at your life through the lens of possibility. When you decide that something is possible, take the necessary steps, even small ones, towards making the possible a reality.
- Remember that all feelings and emotions are temporary. They will pass. Take action to support yourself through the challenging moments, and celebrate every feeling that is good.
- Choose love. Choose love for yourself, and show love to those who are dear to you. A heart filled with love is a beautiful treasure to have and to hold.
- Always look forward. Move forward towards the person you want to become. Do not let who you were, or how you were in the past, hold you back from creating the new and exciting future you long for.

As one of my favourite quotes so eloquently states:

> *"Everything you want lies on the other side of fear."*
>
> *George Addair*

As you near the completion of my book, I want to thank you for maintaining your interest and commitment to read it right to the very end. It is my sincere hope that you have picked up at least one new piece of information, or learned from one idea expressed in a way that inspires you and resonates with you. Perhaps you have used the workbook pages that I have provided. Maybe you have a clearer idea of the values that you now choose to live by. Perhaps you have created a list of belief statements that you recite to yourself with growing conviction each morning, as you look at yourself in your bathroom mirror. Perhaps you have defined your purpose, your mission statement, and your 'reason for being' as you journey forward through life. If you have made a conscious effort to develop a list, create a habit, or more clearly define your purpose, congratulations! Maybe you now practise gratitude in a more considered, regular, and conscious way. If you have taken even one of these steps, you have begun to more fully 'flesh out' your own self-leadership map.

If, on the other hand, you find yourself still sitting on the fence, waiting, telling yourself stories about why making this commitment to yourself is actually too difficult or too time consuming, I urge you to think again. The clock is ticking while you sit frozen in inaction. Your precious time is slipping away while you continue repeating the behaviours and actions that you know, deep inside, no longer serve you. You know, deep in your heart, that these are the behaviours and habits that you'd really love to change. I'd like to remind you that the transformation you seek will not come unless **you take action**. You need to move, try, experiment, change, grow! Transformation begins the moment you realise that:

- A change needs to be made, and only you can make it.
- The application of information is vital. Simply knowing that something is worthwhile and effective, is NOT actually doing something that is worthwhile and effective.
- Taking the first step towards taking action puts you in the driver's seat, as you follow your self-leadership map.

Ever since I realised that I am actually the master of my own destiny, I have felt truly empowered to live my life as the real, authentic me. Sitting alongside these feelings of empowerment, also sits a quiet sense of calm and relief that now resides deep within me. I know that I am on the right path. I know I am living the life I have designed. I know that, when I live from my values and my belief statements, I am the truest, most authentic version of myself. I am proud of my choices. I am happy in my own skin. I am also acutely aware that, whatever happens to me, whatever comes my way in life, I have to make my own decisions, and use my judgement to live as best I can. It is my responsibility to use the tools I know work so well. It is also then my responsibility to do my very best in whatever situation I may find myself.

As I write these words, it is 5.51 am in late December. It is a quiet cool morning and I am enjoying the gentle peace of my house. You may wonder what the day ahead looks like for me. The answer is that my day has already begun.

I have:

- Completed my morning ritual of belief statements, bathroom breaths, reading something uplifting that inspires me, and written in my morning journal where I set my intention for the day.
- Written a small section of the book you now hold in your hands.
- I have planned the rest of my day to include my morning walk, a visit with my mum, the final shopping for our Christmas lunch, and preparations for a Christmas celebration with friends in the evening.
- Prepared my gratitude journal to record three things I am grateful for at the end of this new day.

Ever since I have lived this way, where I complete certain rituals each day, I have found that my life has a rhythm and a flow that feels so comfortable and is truly mine. I find that I am calmer and more centred when I complete my morning ritual. The morning ritual is mine. I designed it and, I am proud to say, I use it to centre and ground myself so that whatever may come my way later in the day, I am better equipped to deal with the problems and challenges that may arise because I know, and accept, that they are inevitable in life.

I believe that my morning ritual is a form of self-appreciation, self-care, and self-love. It doesn't take long to complete but, when it is carried out with my full attention and with an open heart, it sets me up for a truly self-aware and fulfilling day. I know that because I value myself. I am worth the time, energy, and focus it takes to set myself up for success each day.

My message to you is that you are also worth the investment. This investment is one that you must make in yourself. You must invest in every decision you make about how you choose to live your life. You are worth the time, and the energy it takes to love and nurture the beautiful person you are. Think of yourself as a flower. When flowers are nurtured with fresh air, water, and sunlight, they grow, they thrive, and they bloom. When human beings are nurtured with healthy diets, exercise, time for planning, learning, and self-reflection, they also flourish. If we do not choose to honour, nurture and invest in ourselves, how can we expect that others will think we are worthy of their time and attention?

> *"There's always going to be someone who doesn't see your worth. Don't let it be you."*
>
> Mel Robbins

I want to encourage you to celebrate who you are. You are a work of art. You may not feel this way about yourself, and you may feel that others do not respect, treasure and treat you as though you are, but I encourage you to think again. Think of yourself as a 'colour by numbers' picture. You know the ones I mean. The ones that come in a box with the completed image on the cover of the picture you will paint if you follow the rules. The ones where you must follow the guide, and use the paint that matches with the corresponding number in the picture. If you paint by numbers, you will have a perfectly balanced and complete copy that matches the one on the box. A carbon copy!

You are not designed to be a carbon copy of anything or anyone. You are designed to be an original. So, if you were to stop, to think again, and were to actually consider using the colours that you prefer, you will paint the parts of the picture that you would like to highlight and emphasise. You might just surprise yourself by actually creating a masterpiece, an original, a one-off never to be repeated again! Imagine that. You could actually design and paint a picture that fully expresses and celebrates you. Would it be a work of art? Yes. It would be an actual living treasure. There is nothing, in my opinion, more beautiful, and more wonderful, than seeing a person who is living life on their own terms as they strive to become the very best, most complete version of themselves.

Self-Leadership Map Signpost No:7
Turn down fear + turn up self-love + consistent action = Possibility + progress + opportunity.

A Great Coaching Questions About Love and Fear
How is this belief about love/fear serving you?
Has anyone else ever been in a situation like this or are you the first to ever experience it?
If your love was greater than your fear, what would you do next?
If you were giving advice to your closest friend, what would you tell them?

A Piece of Wisdom from Positive Psychology
Love and fear are opposites. Love breeds positive emotions, like joy, peace, and satisfaction. Fear breeds negative emotions, like anger, guilt, and sadness.

Chapter Nine
Thank You! Thank You! Thank You!

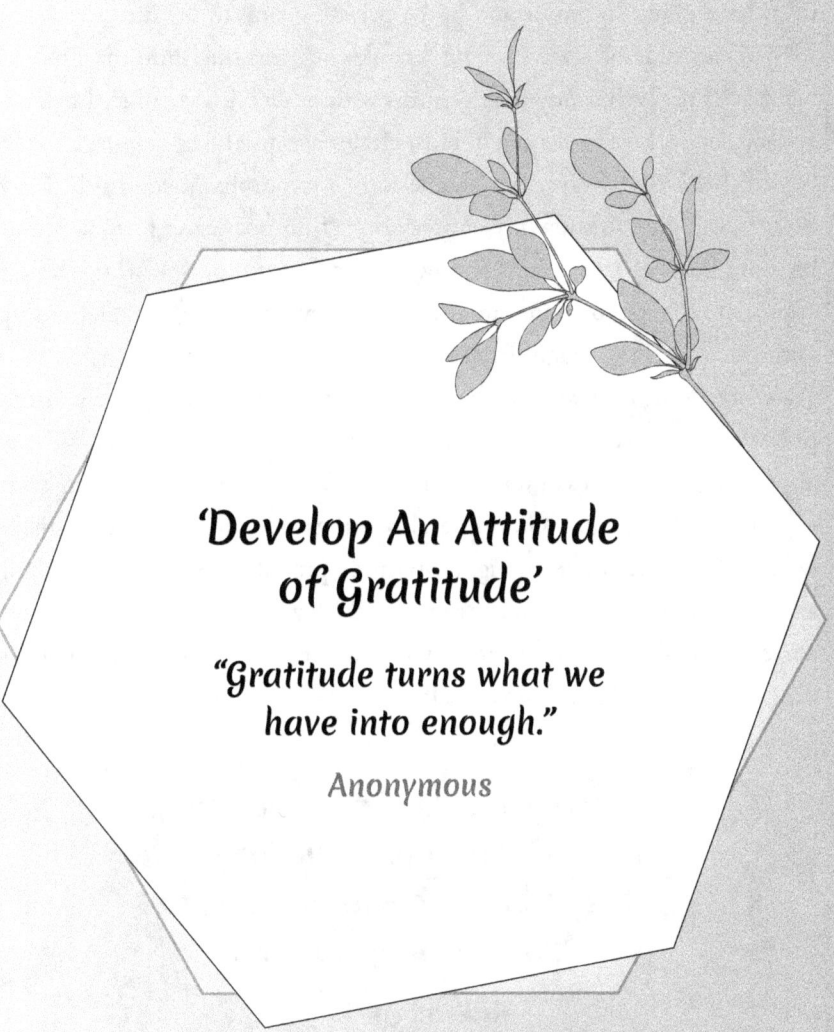

'Develop An Attitude of Gratitude'

"Gratitude turns what we have into enough."

Anonymous

I remember many years ago, when I first experienced the wonders of coaching and living my life through the lens of Positive Psychology, I learned about the practice of gratitude. Was I always a person who said "thank you"? Of course I was! I was well mannered, and well meaning. I had been raised to be a polite and respectful child, who always knew how to 'behave', both in public and in the private realms of my life.

This attitude of always saying "thank you" was bred into my DNA. It has served me well in my relationships with others. I was polite. I behaved appropriately. I was welcome in most circles because I had manners. I knew how to behave. I always said "thank you". I wrote thank you cards. I gave flowers and gifts to show my appreciation. I do not regret for one minute learning how to behave in this way. I'm glad I am a person who is able to appreciate others, to appreciate the things they do for me, my relationships with them, and the magnificence of the world around me.

What I did not realise at the time was the power of a regular gratitude practice. I have learned that what we focus on is what we notice. What we appreciate, appreciates or increases in value. I also learned an amazing secret – gratitude brings joy. Gratitude also brings openness. Gratitude makes what we have seem like enough. Gratitude provides the fuel in your tank, and the power to move you through each day. Becoming a truly grateful person makes you shine. It helps you remain open to see all the good in others, in the world and in yourself.

> *"When you arise in the morning.*
> *Think of what a precious privilege*
> *it is to be alive – to breathe, to*
> *think, to enjoy, to love."*
>
> Marcus Aurelius

I began developing my gratitude practice as a habit when I first learned about it in 2016 while studying for the Certificate in Positive Psychology. The moment I returned from that wonderful course at Geelong Grammar, I began my practice. For the next 165 days, I wrote in my gratitude journal. I did not miss a single day.

It was a simple practice to begin with. At the end of each day, I wrote the date at the top of my page, and then I wrote the following words:

'**Today, I am grateful for**' and then I simply wrote down three things from the day that made me feel thankful. Listed below is an example.

Today I am grateful for:

- *My beautiful family, who makes me smile and feel happy, that they are part of me and I am part of them.*
- *The magnificent autumn sunrise that greeted me this morning as I drove to work.*
- *An opportunity to speak with Jenny, who made me realise how special conversation and connection can be. I felt really seen, appreciated and loved.*

The words of gratitude expressed here are an excerpt from one of my old gratitude journals. You can see that this type of thinking, reflecting, feeling, and writing exercise would only take a few minutes. It is a powerful and extremely calming way to end your day.

I imagine that you may be thinking at this point that, if this practice is so simple and so rewarding, why did I stop writing after 165 days? This is a valid question, and my answer to it is this: I am human; I am often weak; I am sometimes lazy; I sometimes allow myself to go back to old patterns and ways of thinking and being.

I stopped writing my gratitude journal because life got hard. I allowed myself to wallow in what wasn't going so well for me. I let myself focus on all the things that were not showing up in my life as I would have liked them to. I let my inner critic, the negative voice of self-doubt, tell me that gratitude was a waste of time.

Interestingly, after a while I realised that nobody, except for my inner critic and I, were turning up to my self-indulgent pity party. So I stopped, I looked again, and I encouraged myself to step out of the negativity that was getting me nowhere fast. I began writing my journal again. At the time of writing this chapter of my book, I have been consistently writing in my journal for seven years.

I truly believe that using a journal is an excellent start to declaring your gratitude. I believe, even more strongly, that developing an entire gratitude practice is a game changer. Viewing the world through the lens of appreciation provides me with energy, positivity, and hope. I feel wonderful when I choose to view my world in this way.

What is my practice?

*Intention *Expectation *Attention *High Emotion *Gratitude *Expansion

- I always begin my day by setting an **intention**.

Example:

Today, I will take the time to notice all that is beautiful in my world. I will smile when I notice something that stirs me. I will allow the emotion I experience to fill my heart, and I will celebrate the beauty around me by smiling, by sharing my gratitude and joy with my husband. I will notice the small things that make every day special. I am aware and grateful.

- Next, I breathe mindfully and think about all the things I already appreciate in life and all that I **expect** from my day.

Example:

Breathing in, I close my eyes and listen. I hear bird songs and distant traffic.
Breathing out, I say a quiet 'thank you' into my heart.
Breathing in, I think about my body. I think about how my eyes see, my ears hear, my hands feel, my legs walk, my lungs breathe, and my heart beats.
Breathing out, I say a quiet 'thank you' into my heart.

- Next, I give conscious **attention** to my thoughts. I write them down.

  I take my journal and I write whatever comes to me in the next 5 to 10 minutes. Sometimes, I write lists, sometimes, I write phrases and, sometimes, I write in a continuous flow of thoughts, feelings, ideas and emotions.

Example:

April 7, 2023

Gentle rain and bird song. It seems an appropriate way to spend the early part of Good Friday. Sleepy suburb, not many awake. No early morning coffee shop visits today. Lots of time though, time for me. Space to think and create and be. The start of the first term holidays. Time for rest, re-energising and relaxation. Time for me. Creativity flows. Happy, calm, expectant feelings fill me.

- I generate **high emotion** by really feeling the energy and the positivity around the intention I have set for my day.

Example:

I sit with my intention. I walk around my quiet house. I do not disturb my sleeping husband. I look out my window to see a still, grey morning. The daylight has broken through, and everything seems just so peaceful. The incessant chatter of birds reminds me how wonderful it is to be alive! I have this day, this special day, that I will never have again. I promise myself that I will live it to the best of my ability. I will celebrate it with love, joy, laughter and music. I will show through my body that I appreciate all the good things in my life. This appreciation will shine through me. It will make people wonder why I am so happy, vibrant, and positive.

- I practise **gratitude** throughout my day as I see or experience wonderful things. I practise **gratitude** in the evening by writing three things I am grateful for in my gratitude journal.

Often, I experience gratitude when I am out in nature. I may be on my early morning walk. I may be driving east into a magnificent sunrise as I head to school. I often notice things such as: a group of lorikeets flying through the beautiful bushland that surrounds me; a glorious pink sunrise that seems to sit just at the end of a long country road.

I also experience gratitude every day in my work as a primary school principal. One of my greatest joys is doing the morning 'before school' duty. I welcome each and every student. I say hello, I say their names, I speak with parents, I listen to news, I help calm little anxieties, I hear funny stories and jokes, and I celebrate birthdays. These interactions where people feel seen, heard and welcomed, fill my heart and they give me the fuel and the energy to bring my best to the day. I store most of these moments away in my heart, but sometimes I share them with staff or parents. When I do this duty with love and presence, I am filling my own cup with love, with joy, and with a grateful heart for the privilege I have been given.

- I always **expand** my practice by including others. I thank someone new every day by telling them what I appreciate in them or what I am grateful for about them.

I try really hard to pay my gratitude forward. I tell my husband, my mother, one of my siblings, my children, a friend, a colleague or a student, the things I appreciate about them. I share the things I notice that make me feel happy, proud or grateful that they are in my life. If at all possible, I take the time to tell them in person about the things I notice and the things I appreciate. Other ways that I show my gratitude include: sending a text; buying some flowers or a small gift; acknowledging the effort, the growth, and a job well done. It always amazes me how much people are blown away when someone takes the time to acknowledge and really see them.

Gratitude has a ripple effect. When I practise gratitude, it definitely benefits me. I feel big hearted, kind, generous, expansive, and aware. Gratitude also makes the receiver of the thanks, compliment, or feedback, feel seen and appreciated. One strong example I can share about the ripple effect of gratitude and appreciation, is when my staff and I celebrated an end of year Christmas lunch. It was at the end of 2020, a particularly hard year due to the pandemic, and all that had changed so rapidly in our lives.

We decided that our Christmas celebration would take the form of a long lunch at school. A beautiful long table was set, a magnificent spread of food and drink was provided. I could see my staff visibly relax. They were glad to stop. They were grateful to be in each other's company.

Every year at Christmas, I give each staff member a small gift, often a movie ticket that can be used over the summer holidays. I place the ticket, and a Christmas card, in each staff member's pigeon hole in the staff room. They were always appreciative. I was always thanked by many.

This particular year, my Deputy Principal had decided to gather a small collection of handmade, or locally produced items, and to make a gift box for each person. This was a lovely new idea. We really wanted to acknowledge the hard work, flexibility, creativity and agility the staff had demonstrated in providing ongoing education and support to our students as COVID-19 raged across the world.

Towards the end of the lunch, I stood to address the staff. This was nothing unusual. They all knew that I loved to speak. When speaking on my topic, I didn't often require notes. What the staff did not expect was that I would call each staff member individually to receive their gift from my Deputy Principal. I took the time to tell each person what I was grateful for about them, and why I appreciated them on our team.

It was quite amazing! The silence was palpable. Every member of our team sat silent and attentive as I spoke about each person and their qualities, their efforts, their acts of teamwork, generosity, and kindness. I did not realise the full impact of publicly sharing my gratitude for each person, until I was approached by staff member after staff member who said that they were blown away by the way I acknowledged each person's contribution and gifts.

> "At times our own light goes out and is rekindled by a spark from another person. Each one of us has cause to think with deep gratitude for those who have lighted the flame within us."
>
> Albert Schweitzer

Over the school holidays, I found myself reflecting on what had happened at that Christmas lunch, and on the feedback I'd received. I felt good. I felt proud, and I felt acknowledged. I realised that these were the same emotions that each staff member experienced when I expressed my gratitude for them. I realised that the gratitude I had expressed that day had caused expansive ripples of love and emotion that reached all the way back to me. I also knew that what I had wholeheartedly expressed had returned to warm my heart, to further build my confidence, and to assure me that what we express in gratitude always returns in ways we don't always expect. Here is my journal entry from that day:

14.12.20

Today I am grateful for:

- The joy and beauty of our shared staff celebration.
- The new realisation that, when I publicly and spontaneously acknowledge my colleagues for their personal qualities and contributions, it is very powerful and amazingly moving.
- The realisation that the practice of appreciation, and taking the time to notice the things that make people special, is actually a magical gift for both the giver and the receiver.

When I speak with others about my particular practice of gratitude, and the daily recording of the things for which I am grateful, people often ask me about the really hard days, the empty days, the sad days, the days where it feels as though nothing goes to plan. They ask me how I find something to be grateful for on those days. I always respond with the same answer. I tell them that, on those days, I look a little harder. I search a little deeper. I reflect a little more. Often the hard days occur because my expectations are, as I mentioned previously, not being met either by myself or by others. On those days, when I search for the lesson, I ask myself, "What did I learn through this truly challenging day?"

One way to further explain this idea is to share a recent life experience. In September 2023 I was extremely fortunate to have the opportunity to travel with a group of my fellow principals to Spain. On this trip, we were going to walk part of the Camino, or the St James Walk as it is also known. For many hundreds of years, people from all over the world have embarked on this physical, mental, and spiritual pilgrimage. As a group, guided by our spiritual director, we were going to walk 120 kms over six days.

I had trained for the experience by walking every morning, and sometimes again in the evening. I had completed some long-distance walks in the weeks leading up to my adventure. I had all the correct gear for the trip – hiking shoes, special socks, walking clothes, walking poles, backpack, etc. I was excited, more apprehensive than I wanted to admit, but definitely inspired, looking forward to the journey ahead and was ready to go.

The day of the walk dawned. It was September 7, 2023. I was about to start a physical and spiritual challenge that I knew would be difficult in parts, but I was ready. I had shared with my school community the preparations I had made for the walk, and I had promised our students that I would email and send photos daily to let them share the journey with me.

THANK YOU! THANK YOU! THANK YOU!

We gathered as a group in a small courtyard space on that cool and beautiful morning. We shared a moving reflection and a prayer. We wished each other 'Buen Camino' and then we set off. Each of us soon found a group with whom we felt socially connected and comfortable, or we found a group that seemed to walk at a pace that matched our fitness level. I walked with three other women, and we chatted as we walked along the path through the stunningly beautiful countryside of Sarria, in northern Spain. It soon became evident to me that it was going to be a very hot day, and the challenge of walking 20 km was going to be a massive one. I very quickly realised that my personal challenge was going to be the many steep hills that lay between me and my destination.

As we walked on, my discomfort quickly grew. Was I unwell? Did I have a virus? I was unsure. My main concern was the way I struggled for breath as I walked the stony paths, uneven surfaces, and the seemingly endless sharp inclines and declines I was asking my body to navigate. I found myself looking for the flat parts of the path so that I could regain some sense of composure and equilibrium. After struggling for quite some time, I let my ego get in the way. I didn't like the thought of my colleagues watching me struggle in this way. I told them to go on without me. I told them that I was feeling a little unwell, and that I didn't want to hold them up. The fact is, I was feeling extremely unwell. I said I'd just go at my own pace. They spent some time discussing this with me before agreeing to go on ahead.

After they left me, I sat down to catch my breath, wipe the sweat from my face, and to drink some water that contained electrolytes. I got up to resume my walk. I knew that I didn't feel at all well. Did I have a virus? Was it the food I'd eaten the previous night? Who knew? Did I allow myself to become dehydrated and overwhelmed by the physical challenge? To this day, I will never know for sure.

I dragged myself up hills and down the other side. I walked through the small clusters of houses that punctuated the path. As I did this, I became increasingly unwell. The heat and nausea played havoc with my mindset. I was really struggling. My inner critic was working overtime as she told me to quit. She also filled my head with thoughts about what my colleagues would think of me, and constantly reinforced the notion that I just wasn't good enough. My thoughts vacillated between keeping going for my ego's sake and quitting because I really couldn't go much further.

The pathway of the Camino is beautiful, challenging in many parts and, sometimes, surprising where you least expect it. As I stumbled and struggled along the path feeling wretched and hopeless, it opened out to a small group of houses nestled together. The homes were simple, humble and, obviously, very much loved.

As I drew close to the houses, I saw what must have been a common domestic scene. The elderly residents of three of the houses were engaged in deep and animated conversation. One old lady was sweeping her front verandah, another was joining in whilst hanging out of her upstairs window and, finally, there was an old couple sitting in the Spanish sunshine enjoying what was obviously a daily ritual.

As I stumbled along the path, I was unaware of the fact that the old woman sitting on the verandah with her husband had noticed my struggle. She had no English, and I had no Spanish. She gestured to me and said something in Spanish that I interpreted as 'Slowly, slowly'. I gave her a weak smile and stumbled on. She then surprised me by gesturing for me to sit in the vacant chair on their verandah.

If I had not been so desperate, and so unwell, I would have thanked her and kept going but, on this day, I knew that I needed a rest. I sat in silence and tried to rest and regroup. I probably spent fifteen minutes in the company of these beautiful Spanish seniors who simply allowed me to be.

After a while, I knew I needed to move again. I slowly stood and smiled with my eyes and gestured my gratitude to the beautiful lady who had offered me respite. I had no words to share with her, but I like to think that she sensed my deep appreciation of her kindness. I had just shared a beautiful moment of communion with another human being. In this moment, I felt truly blessed.

As I pushed on, I was aware that I was moving at an extraordinarily slow pace. I stopped many times. Nausea overtook me, and I found myself vomiting, struggling with stomach cramps and the associated discomforts. I stopped drinking as I didn't want to continue to vomit. At one stage, I left the path and wandered into the trees off the side of the road to vomit yet again, I became entangled in blackberry canes. As I worked to disentangle myself from this prickly and painful mess, I realised my ankles were scratched and bleeding. I kept asking myself, how much worse could things get? I must have looked 'a sight' as I walked very slowly, and sometimes stumbled along the seemingly endless path under the relentless Spanish sun.

I knew I was still a long way from my destination. I was feeling disoriented, exhausted and hopeless. My phone rang in my backpack. It was our spiritual director and guide. He was checking in because he had learned from my colleagues that I was walking alone. I told him that I was feeling quite unwell. He quizzed me about my location on the endless Camino path. He told me to walk to a certain point and that he would walk back to meet me. He reassured me that we would walk the rest of the way together. I crossed a main highway and sat slumped at the corner just as I was instructed. I felt weak, sick, disoriented and hopeless.

When our guide arrived, he looked at me and told me that I would walk no further that day. He told me that he thought I'd better go by taxi to the hotel, have a shower, start to re-hydrate, and sleep. I did not have the strength to argue. In many ways, I was grateful to have the decision not to go on taken from me. I numbly went through the motions of showering, drinking water, and falling into my hotel bed. Never did a clean body, clean sheets, and a pillow feel so good. I slept for many, many hours, and awoke the next morning a little worse for wear, feeling quite insecure about facing my colleagues but ready to face the path again. Surely, I would do better today!

You may wonder what I recorded in my gratitude journal on this particularly challenging day. At this stage of my life, my journal writing followed the following process:

- Record the date in my journal.
- Write whatever thoughts come to mind, always starting with the word, 'Today'.
- Write a reflection on my experiences, and record at least three things I am grateful for on that day.

Here is an excerpt from my journal after my first day walking from Sarria to Portomarin (written the following morning due to condition):

7.9.23

Today is the first day of my walk on 'The Way'. I am excited, hopeful, and scared all at once. I am open to seeing what the day brings. I will make it up the 'hill' that scares me so much. I will walk. I will breathe. I will grow.

Today I am grateful for:

- *Making a start to my walk.*
- *Learning more about myself – my fears, my courage, my self-awareness, my need to always appear in control.*

THANK YOU! THANK YOU! THANK YOU!

- *The Spanish woman who showed me such deep kindness, care and respect.*
- *My kind and generous spiritual director and guide.*
- *Clean sheets, a comfortable bed, and the welcome gift of sleep.*

As I mentioned previously, sometimes when reflecting on my day, and searching for some things to record in my journal, I struggle. I ask myself, *"What was good about today?"* On some days, it can be really challenging to think about anything except the things that didn't go my way. Sometimes, I have to really dig deep to remember something beautiful that I had noticed in nature. Sometimes I have to challenge myself to remember a kind word, a smile, or a funny moment from a really challenging day. Often, I have to simply search for the lesson and ask myself reflective questions, such as:

- What did I learn about myself and other people today?
- What did I like about myself today?
- What do I know now that I didn't know at the beginning of the day?
- What lesson can I take from today?
- What will I try to do differently tomorrow?

You may wonder after my challenging first day on the Camino just how I went with the remainder of my walk. I am proud to tell you that each day, I did better than the day before and, by the end of my third day, I actually began to find my equilibrium. By the end of the third day, I wasn't just looking at my feet as I determinedly put one foot in front of the other. By the end of the third day, I could actually look up and see the sky and the amazing view of the beautiful Spanish countryside.

I feel it is appropriate to share with you my gratitude journal entry from the final day of the walk:

13.9.23

Today is the final day of my walk. Who knew that I would write those words with a mixture of relief, joy, and pride?

I will participate in whatever the day delivers me. I will enjoy each moment as a treasured gift.

Today I am grateful for:

- *Completion*
- *Achievement*
- *The dazzling sight of the cathedral at Santiago*
- *Many treasured gifts*
- *My walking companion*

At the completion of the Camino, I was extremely proud of myself because I had stuck with the process. I had completed the journey. I had achieved what I came to Spain to achieve. I had the experience of a lifetime. I had used every ounce of courage and dogged determination I possessed in order to complete my pilgrimage. At the conclusion of the walk, I felt proud and satisfied. I felt elated. I had completed what, for me, was a great physical challenge. I had learned more about who I was as a person. I came to realise that, as we live our lives and encounter whatever challenges may arise, we can enjoy the encouragement and support of other people but, ultimately, we walk our journeys alone. We must develop our own strategies and methods for living. We must rely on our own self-leadership maps to navigate the highs and lows of our journey through life.

> "Instead of saying, 'Have to do this'.
> Say, 'Get to do this'.
> Everything is a privilege."
>
> Sonya Looney

The practice of gratitude has truly changed my life. I have certainly developed the now deeply ingrained habit of recording my thoughts, feelings, and expressions of gratitude in my journal. But far more importantly than that, I realise that, as I live and breathe each day, I know I am more aware of the people and the things that surround me. Not only am I more aware, I know I have become a person who is wired to appreciate even the smallest things that are beautiful, meaningful, and worthwhile in my life.

As the anonymous quote at the beginning of this chapter so elegantly states, "Gratitude turns what we have into enough".

My strong suggestion to you, as you read my book, is to buy yourself a journal, a simple book with blank pages on which to write. Begin simply by recording three things for which you are truly thankful. Make this a part of your ritual as you end your day and prepare to sleep. This act places you into a restorative and grateful space, so that you can prepare to rest and restore yourself. You can then face the new day with courage and full appreciation.

Self-Leadership Map Signpost No:8
Self-respect + recognition of opportunity + life choices + healthy habits = gratitude + growth + self-pride + progress.

Great Coaching Questions About Gratitude
What's a hard lesson that you were grateful to learn?
What about today has been better than yesterday?
What's an aspect of your physical health that you feel grateful for?
What happened today/yesterday/this week/this month/this year that you're grateful for?

A Piece of Wisdom from Positive Psychology
Gratitude helps people feel more positive emotions, relish good experiences, improve their health, deal with adversity, and build strong relationships

Chapter Ten
Eye on the Prize

'Produce and direct the movie of a lifetime – you are the star!'

"Everyone has a purpose in life and a unique talent to give to others. And when we blend this unique talent with service to others, we experience the ecstasy and exultation of our own spirit, which is the ultimate goal of all goals."

Kallam Anji Reddy

The following words are the words that drive me these days. These are the words that cause me to strive to grow and develop myself further each and every day. *"I want to inspire and help women old and young to realise their own self-worth, potential and power through brave self-leadership. I want them to know that they are neither too young nor too old and that it is never too early nor too late to start."*

It seems to me that, whether we realise it or not, we spend so much of our lives searching. We spend time searching for who we want to be in the world, and for ways to authentically show up. We want to connect with others, we want to be included and accepted and, above all, we want to feel as though we belong.

As I reflect on my life, I see the many stages of learning, struggle and growth, as I worked to understand who I was and how I wanted to be perceived in the world. As a teenager, I did what most do. I saw people I admired or aspired to be like, and then worked at trying my best to belong to their group, or to emulate their style. This is normal human behaviour.

In my endeavours to work out who I was, I became an excellent mimic. I tried on new fashions, new ways of speaking, new interests, new eating and lifestyle habits. I guess that most of us can identify with trying to find 'our tribe' when we were adolescents or young adults. This is how we learn and grow. I have only to look back at old photos that trace the styles and stages of my life, to realise that this was all part of becoming the woman I am today.

> *"Having a purpose is the difference between making a living and making a life."*
> Tom Thiss

When I look back over my life so far, with the benefit of hindsight, there is one thing that is most evident, I have always had an ability to communicate and to connect deeply with people. During all of the stages of my life, these skills and talents have allowed me to, most often, be included and accepted wherever I have gone in the world. As I grew older, and was so strongly drawn to, and inspired by the work of teaching, leadership, personal development and coaching, so much of what I instinctively knew made perfect sense to me. Once I learned that my values and beliefs helped me steer my life in a positive and productive direction, I found that articulating my purpose became a driving force for me. I fully realised what I had always, in essence, known. I am a communicator, a connector, a writer, and a coach.

In my chosen career as a teacher, I have used these communication skills to connect with my students, their parents, and with my colleagues. I have always been able to move comfortably among a wide variety of people. This, I realise, is because I use my character strengths of love, kindness, social intelligence, and perspective, in my daily interactions. I also use my God-given talent of communication to connect with others.

As my career progressed and I became a principal, I have had many opportunities to lead, to guide, to coach, and to connect with others. I came to realise the unique privilege it is to work in this role. The moment I understood that I had the tools, and the language, to support people in their personal and professional journeys, I knew that this way of thinking, working and communicating, was what I wanted to do with the rest of my life. I had found my purpose, and my reason for being. I also realised that I had been doing this work for many years through my professional interactions with teachers, students and parents and, far more informally, among my friends and within my family.

The day I fully realised that a deep connection with others was the most important and inspiring element of my life's work, it was also the day I realised that I could be more than one iteration of myself at a time. I came to understand that writing, speaking, and coaching, can sit harmoniously alongside my precious work as a principal. It became clear that I did not have to choose between one career and another. At this stage of my life, I could successfully combine both. It became very clear that leading and supporting the people within my sphere of influence at school was not only a valid and essential part of my role, but also a natural expression of who I am as a woman. I came to understand that writing a book, speaking about my work, and working with private coaching clients, was the 'side hustle', the 'Plan B' that I hope will become more as I grow into the next phase of my life.

> *"Discovering your purpose is the most significant thing you will do in your life, and you, your loved ones, and the world will be better off because you went on this journey."*
>
> Mastin Kipp

Spending time writing this book has caused me to reflect deeply on my life's journey up to this point. It has also shone a bright and unwavering light on who I want to be in the world as I move forward. I have felt a deep calling to, once again, clarify and state my purpose. I realised that my writing has a strongly feminine voice. I have seen so many women of all ages hold themselves back because of circumstance, because the timing wasn't right, because they put themselves last, and because they didn't see that small steps made with encouragement and support can often be the biggest steps they will ever take in their lives. I realised that my purpose was to lend my voice to the growing chorus of people who want to inspire women of all ages to step into their personal power, and live their best lives each and every day.

I want women to know that they can start from wherever they are, and use whatever resources they have available to them. I want to send a message to all women that they are important. I want them to know that they are worth their own investment in self-care, time, resources, and self-respect. I want them to know they have so much to give, and to share with the world. I want them to know that they deserve to live lives that are rich, enjoyable, and fulfilling. I want them to know that they can take action to be in the driver's seat of their own destinies. I want them to live lives they can be truly proud of.

I distinctly remember being in conversation one day with a woman, named Colleen Callander, who had worked with me and with my leadership team at school. She had a brilliant career as the C.E.O of Sportsgirl, from which she had recently retired. She was doing many of the things I aspire to do. She had written and published a book. She had offers to speak at events, and she had developed programs and retreats where she could coach, mentor, and inspire other women. I was so impressed by what she had done. She was doing exactly what I was aspiring to do.

After I expressed my dreams, desires, and future plans to her, she asked me a question that resonated deeply within me. I carried this question around with me for months. She asked what my essential message was. I looked at her quizzically, not exactly sure what she was asking me. She elaborated by asking whether I could define my purpose in a statement that I could deliver in a 'nutshell', or an essential statement that I could deliver with confidence and conviction. She stressed the utmost importance of being able to deliver a statement that clearly defines your purpose, your passion, your reason for being, your 'why' in a clear, engaging, and succinct manner. She also told me that she believed that my published book would be the most precious 'business card' that I could ever hold in my hand.

I moved on from that meeting with an inspired mind, and an excited heart. I worked diligently to define my statement. I took a number of steps that helped me to clearly articulate my purpose. Written below is the process I undertook. I asked myself the following questions, and I wrote answers to these questions over and over again until I had refined my answer. These are the questions I asked myself:

1. Who am I?
2. What do I want to achieve?
3. Who do I want to inspire, encourage, affect, and support?
4. What is my message, my statement to the world?
5. What will be my legacy?

I worked to answer these questions over a period of days until I felt that I had nailed what would be my 'elevator pitch'. I also decided that an 'elevator pitch' was merely a clever name to help me capture and clearly define my purpose. What I had actually written was my mission statement. The defining statement that would guide my direction, my work, and my purpose for years to come.

My answers to these questions went something like this:

1. **Who am I?**

    I am a woman, a wife, a mother, a grandmother, a daughter, a sister, a friend, a teacher, a principal, a writer, a speaker, a coach, a sensitive, and at times, complex woman.

2. **What do I want to achieve?**
   I want to speak, coach, write, and lead. I want to make a living from doing this work. I want to express and fulfil my heart's longing to step completely into this field of work.

3. **Who do I want to inspire, encourage, affect and support?**
   I want to connect with, and empower, women of all ages to believe in themselves. I want to inspire and empower them to listen to, and use, their intuition, their innate wisdom, and their feminine qualities, attributes and strengths, to build lives that follow their self-leadership maps – lives they can find fulfilling and be truly proud of.

4. **What is my message, my statement to the world?**
   My message to the world is: "Women, don't wait! Don't try to do it alone! Reach out. Seek support. Connect with, and support others. Together, we are stronger!"

5. **What will be my legacy?**
   My legacy will be the part I played in helping women discover their own unique purpose and power. Through this work, I will have contributed to making the world a better, more caring, more supportive, and kinder place. My legacy will be the ripple effect that I have begun, by authentically living my purpose and assisting and supporting women of all ages to live theirs.

So, I hear you ask, did you develop your elevator pitch, your mission statement? Did you define your purpose? Did you find your 'why'?

In answer to these questions, it is important to answer 'Yes'. I feel assured and strong in my identity. I have certainty around what I want to achieve.

I know, from the depths of my heart, that I want to inspire, encourage and support other women to flourish and to become the very best version of themselves.

My message to the world is that I care deeply about the self-confidence of women, and that I want to inspire and skill them in developing strong and effective self-leadership maps.

My legacy will be a body of work that clearly demonstrates that I walked my talk, and that I connected deeply with, and inspired others, to strive, to learn, and to grow, so that they can live rich, full and rewarding lives.

In reading the pages of my book, and working through the learning tasks I have set in the workbook spaces provided, it is my sincere hope that you are developing a clearer, stronger picture of who you are, and who you aspire to be. You may find it useful to complete the chart below, to provide yourself with answers to the questions I asked myself. Take the time to answer these questions, and then reflect on your responses over the coming days. See if the woman you describe is the woman you aspire to be. Think about one or two small actions that you can take immediately, to begin to become that woman, and set yourself on the journey of a lifetime. Remember small positive actions, repeated daily, will produce consistent and sustainable progress and change over time.

Question	Response
Who am I?	
What do I want to achieve?	
Who do I want to encourage, inspire, affect, and support?	
What is my message, my statement to the world?	
What will be my legacy?	

Self-Leadership Map Signpost No:9
Wanting a better result = Asking a better question.

Great Coaching Questions About Vision, Mission and Purpose
Review the year so far, what's going well for you? What's not working?
What are you like when you're at your best? What are you doing?
If you saw yourself in three years time living the same life, how would that feel?
If you could be a role model to yourself, what would you do?

A Piece of Wisdom from Positive Psychology
Research in the area of positive psychology explains that people with a purpose in life live longer, have a better immune system, and perform better, even when one controls for things such as lifestyle, personality, and other factors relating to longevity.

Chapter Eleven
Celebrate You

You Are a Work of Art

"You yourself, as much as anybody in the universe, deserve your love and affection."

Buddha

As you reach the end of this book, I want to express my heartfelt gratitude for your commitment to stay with me to the very last page. I sincerely hope that, throughout this journey, you've gained at least one new insight, one idea that sparked inspiration or resonated deeply within you. Perhaps you've engaged with the workbook exercises, or maybe you now have a clearer sense of the values you choose to live by. Maybe you've crafted belief statements that empower you each morning as you look in the mirror, or define your mission and purpose, as you move forward in life. If you've taken any of these steps, however small, congratulations! You've begun to map your path to stronger self-leadership.

But if you find yourself still hesitating, still making excuses, still stuck in old patterns, I urge you to reconsider. Time is slipping away and, with each moment you remain stagnant, you're reinforcing the behaviours that no longer serve you. Deep down, you know what needs to change, and you know that change cannot happen unless you take action. Transformation requires movement. It requires the courage to try, to experiment, to evolve.

Change begins the moment you realise:

- A shift is necessary, and you are the only one who can make it.
- Knowledge alone is not enough; it's the action behind the knowledge that creates real, lasting impact.
- The first step you take, no matter how small, is the moment you reclaim control of your life and step into your own power.

So, if you've been waiting for the perfect moment, know that the time is now. Begin, even if it's messy. Your self-leadership journey starts the moment you make the choice to move. Don't wait another day. Step forward. The life you want is waiting for you. Take the reins and make a start.

> "Self-leadership is the practice of understanding who you are, identifying your desired experiences, and intentionally guiding yourself toward them. It spans the determination of what we do, why we do it, and how we do it."
>
> *Psychology Today*

Transformation begins the moment you realise that:

- A change needs to be made, and that only you can make it.
- Knowing that something is worthwhile, and effective, is NOT actually DOING something that is worthwhile and effective.
- Taking the first action step puts you in the driver's seat, as you follow your self- leadership map, and your plan for living a life where you are in control.

Ever since I realised that I am actually the master of my own destiny, I have felt truly empowered to live my life as the real, authentic me. Sitting alongside these feelings of empowerment, is a quiet sense of calm and relief that now lives deep within me. I know that I am on the right path. I know I am living the life I have designed. I know that, when I live from my values and from my belief statements, I am the truest, most authentic version of myself. I am proud of my choices. I am happy in my own skin. I am also acutely aware that, whatever happens to me, whatever comes my way in life, it is up to me to make my own decisions, and use my judgement to live my life as best I can. It is my responsibility to use the tools that I know work so well. It is also then my responsibility to do my very best.

As I write these words, it is a quiet, cool morning and I am enjoying the gentle peace of my house. You may wonder what the day ahead looks like for me. The answer is that my day has already begun.

I have:

- Completed my morning ritual of belief statements, bathroom breaths, reading something uplifting that inspires me, and writing in my journal where I set my intention for the day.
- Completed the final check of my manuscript before submitting it for typesetting by the publisher
- I have planned the rest of my day to include my morning walk, coffee with my husband and friends, a catch up with family and an easy, relaxing evening
- Prepared my gratitude journal to record three things I am grateful for from this new day.

Ever since I have lived this way, where I complete certain rituals each day, I have found that my life has a rhythm and a flow that feels natural, comfortable, and truly mine. I find that I am calmer, and more centred, when I set up and complete my morning ritual. The morning ritual is mine. I designed it and, I am proud to say, use it to centre and ground myself so that whatever may come my way later in the day, I am better equipped to deal with problems and challenges that may arise because I know, and accept, that they are inevitable in life.

I believe that my morning ritual is a form of self-appreciation, self-care, and self-love. It doesn't take long to complete but, when it is carried out with my full attention, and with an open heart, it sets me up for a truly self-aware and fulfilling day. I know these things are vital because I truly value myself. I am worth the time, energy, and focus it takes to set myself up for success each day.

> "We are each gifted in a unique and important way. It is our privilege and our adventure to discover our own special light."
> Mary Dunbar

My message to you is that you are also worth the investment. This investment is one that you must make in yourself. Only you can invest in every decision you make about how you choose to live your life. You are worth the time and the energy it takes to love and nurture the beautiful person you are. Think of yourself as a flower. When flowers are nurtured with fresh air, water, and sunlight, they grow, they thrive, and they bloom. When human beings are nurtured with healthy diets, exercise, time for planning, action, and then self-reflection and the practice of gratitude, they also flourish. If we do not choose to honour, nurture and invest in ourselves, how can we expect that others will think we are worthy of their time and attention?

This chapter is titled, 'Celebrate You. You Are a Work of Art.' You may not feel this way about yourself, and may feel that others do not respect, treasure, and treat you as though you are, but I encourage you to think again. Think of yourself as a 'colour by numbers' picture. You know the ones I mean. The ones that come in a box with the completed image on the cover of the picture you will paint if you follow the rules. The ones where you must follow the guide and use the paint that matches with the corresponding number in the picture. If you paint by numbers, you will have a perfectly balanced and complete painting that matches the one on the box. A carbon copy! If you were to think again, and were to consider using the colours that you prefer, and painting the parts of the picture that you would like to highlight and emphasise, you might surprise yourself by actually creating a masterpiece, an original, a one off never to be repeated again! Imagine that. You could actually design and paint a picture that fully expresses and celebrates you. Would it be a work of art? Yes. It would be an actual living treasure. There is nothing, in my opinion, more beautiful and more wonderful than seeing a person who is living life on their own terms, as they strive to become the very best, most complete version of themselves.

Self-Leadership Map Signpost No:10
Knowledge + action + self-reflection + further action = growth + progress + achievement + self-respect + self-love.

Great Coaching Questions About Self-Appreciation
What have I done well today?
How can I honour my needs more?
What makes me feel loved, and how can I give this to myself?
What do I need to forgive myself for?
What would I tell a good friend who was struggling to appreciate themselves?

A Piece of Wisdom from Positive Psychology
Self-appreciation not only boosts your confidence but also helps you to improve and get better day by day. Self-appreciation is the best aspect for success in your life. If you want to succeed then love yourself first. If you want self-appreciation, then love yourself, love your decision, and love your work.

A Final Word of Encouragement

'You Are Your Most
Important Project'

"It takes half your life before you
discover life is a do-it-yourself project."

Napoleon Hill

In these final pages of my book, I want to clearly emphasise my belief that the sooner you realise that no-one is coming to design you, to create you, or to save you, the sooner you can begin to design and live your life on your own terms. You can do this by creating and using your own well-designed, and well-planned, self-leadership map.

I'd like you to imagine for a moment that you are a project manager. You have been offered an extremely important, and highly specialised project. It is to be a 'one off' creation. In your project, you are going to take something that already exists, and you are required to renovate and refine it to showcase its finest features, and to utilise its greatest attributes and skills. You are in charge. It is your responsibility to deliver a first-class product. The project will take careful planning, a great deal of time, dedication, energy, and focus. You may require expert advice and support along the way, which you can elect to obtain from a variety of people, such as coaches, counsellors, mentors, and trusted friends but, ultimately, you know that you are responsible for the delivery of the final product. When the project title is revealed to you, it is the most deeply personal and intimate piece of work that you will ever invest your time and energy in. The project, when finally revealed, is called 'Project You'. You are charged with designing a life plan for yourself. You realise that you are ultimately responsible for shaping the life you live. You realise the enormous honour, responsibility, and privilege you have been given.

When you come to fully understand your personal responsibility for your own life outcomes, you begin to understand that self-love, and effective self-leadership, are the constantly important choices that only you can make. Self-love, and self-leadership, take consistent commitment and effort. They only work effectively when you choose to make a commitment to your boundaries, your wellbeing, and to your physical, mental, emotional, and spiritual health.

This commitment is about developing the self-discipline and self-leadership to shut out the unresourceful voices that are sometimes at play in your head. It is equally important to shut out the voices of others that tell you that it is all too hard, not enough fun, and not worth the consistent effort required to strive for the things you really want. When you find yourself stuck in a rut of unresourceful thinking and living, you can easily become discouraged and convince yourself that the way in which you currently live is the only way forward. You feel stuck. You do not need to stay this way. You are not an unresourceful person. You have simply allowed yourself to fall into a way of thinking, and living, that does not really serve your true needs, or your desire for a more fulfilling and rewarding way of life.

> *"As I began to love myself, I found that anguish and emotional suffering were only warning signs that I was living against my own truth."*
>
> Charlie Chaplin

Now I want to take you on another journey into the world of your imagination. Imagine for a moment that you find yourself in a huge warehouse. It is completely dark, and you cannot see anything at all. All you know is who you are, and how you have lived your life up to this point. The darkness of the warehouse is a wonderful metaphor for the darkness of the worry, confusion, boredom, and indecision you can often experience. You have a tiny torch as your only light source. When you turn it on, the small light beam only allows you to see what is directly in front of you. Your initial thought leads you to believe that what you can see directly in front of you, is the only option or choice you have.

What you have failed to remember in this moment, where your options and choices feel extremely limited, is the power of slowing down, the power of becoming mindful and self-aware, the power of the breath and the power of calmly stated belief statements. By choosing to slow down, and to give yourself time to think again, you will often see things differently. By thinking differently, you will realise that you always have more than one choice available to you. You will also realise that not making a choice and remaining stuck, is actually still a choice.

When you allow yourself to engage in more resourceful and powerful thinking, you take charge and begin to set yourself free. In that moment, it is as though someone has flipped the master switch in the mental warehouse in which you find yourself. All of a sudden, all the lights are on, all the choices are laid out for you to see! Often the shelves are laden with the choices you can make, the next steps you can take. Often all you need to do is slow down, connect with your breath, and think about what you value most, and what you believe about the highest version of yourself.

In these mindful moments, where you choose to take charge, you can actually step into your own personal power. You realise that only you can take positive steps in the direction of your dreams. In that moment, you move closer to skilfully following your own self-leadership map. In that moment, you more fully realise that your life is in your hands. You are the master director. You can create the movie of a lifetime. It really is all up to you. I wish you strength, love, and positivity, as you use the self-leadership map you have designed. I wish you the best on your journey towards your own brilliant life.

About the author

As a woman who has navigated life's challenges, Sue Carr entered the field of education later than most. This unique path has fueled her commitment to personal growth and to supporting others to believe that change is possible. As a mother, grandmother, teacher, well-being specialist, trained coach and a primary school principal, working in a leadership position, she has dedicated her career to empowering individuals through the principles of Positive Psychology. Her mission is to inspire growth, resilience, and the inspiration to create lasting change in those with whom she connects.

Sue has a natural gift for connecting, speaking and presenting, engaging audiences with a blend of naturalness, warmth, vulnerability and positive enthusiasm. She shares actionable steps for personal growth and change that resonates deeply with diverse groups: from school leaders, teachers and learning support staff, to parents and the wider community beyond.

www.ingramcontent.com/pod-product-compliance
Lightning Source LLC
LaVergne TN
LVHW051559070426
835507LV00021B/2658